PREACHING EFFECTIVELY, REVITALIZING YOUR CHURCH

PREACHING EFFECTIVELY, REVITALIZING YOUR CHURCH

The Seven-Step Ladder toward Successful Homilies

GUERRIC DeBONA, OSB

Paulist Press
New York/Mahwah, NJ

Cover design by Joy Taylor
Book design by Sharyn Banks

Library of Congress Cataloging-in-Publication Data

DeBona, Guerric, 1955–
    Preaching effectively, revitalizing your church : the seven-step ladder toward successful homilies / Guerric DeBona.
            p. cm.
    Includes bibliographical references (p.   ).
    ISBN 978-0-8091-4602-4 (alk. paper)
1. Catholic preaching. I. Title.
    BX1795.P72D43 2009
    251´.01—dc22

                                                                    2009031256

 Published by Paulist Press
997 Macarthur Boulevard
Mahwah, New Jersey 07430

www.paulistpress.com

Printed and bound in the
United States of America

CONTENTS

Contents

For Fr. Joe Weigman and Dr. Rick Stern,
who preach by word and example

PREFACE

If you are scanning the beginning of this book, you might be asking the following questions: Why another book on preaching? What difference will it make? Who has the time to read it?

There are some good texts available on making homilies better. Some of them offer great advice about how to tell a good story (William Bausch), or how to stick to a point (Ken Untener), or what defines the homily (Robert Waznak). More books are available on how to improve preaching than ever before. More workshops are held at convocations on homiletics than there has ever been. Preaching services on the Internet abound. Yet if the proliferation of these books on preaching has made any difference, you certainly wouldn't know it by the numbers—or lack thereof—in Catholic churches. The new survey published in February 2008 by the Pew Forum on Religion and Public Life says that the number of Catholics are shrinking—and fast. "Catholicism has experienced the greatest net losses as a result of affiliation changes. While nearly one in three Americans were raised in the Catholic faith, today fewer than one in four describe themselves as Catholic."* So what difference has all of these homily hints and helps made in the long run?

As for the time to spend reading such books…Having been involved with seminary education for over twenty years, I can

---

*The report can be accessed at http://religions.pewforum.org/reports.

say that the priests that I know are among the busiest people in the workforce, what with parish closings or clusterings, school issues, sacraments, financial concerns…The list goes on and on. Is there even a spare hour to read a book that may not make a whole lot of difference anyway?

This book is different. There is nothing to memorize. No catchy theorems to grab the congregation. This book is different because everything in it affirms *what is already in place in the life of the preacher and wants to make it better*: relationship.

In creating a Seven-Step Ladder for Preaching, I take a holistic view, while offering practical and timely suggestions. I want to deal with the question of essentials: What are the key factors that, taken together, lead to success as a preacher?

Let's face it. While there have been myriad recommendations for improving life at the ambo, Catholic homiletics has lacked a series of building blocks for preaching, a kind of method that would find its footing in a triangular arrangement among preacher, text, and assembly. I see the homily, then, as an integrating moment that begins with a foundational relationship with God and God's people. For example, I suggest that the First Step on the Ladder of Preaching is "Discovering a Personal Theology of Preaching." What could be more foundational than to ask *why* we preach? And what do priests, deacons, and other Christian ministers do every day of their lives? They build and discover relationships with God, parish, and the world around them. Preaching cannot be separated from this personal context, indeed from the graced reality in which we find ourselves day after day.

Therefore, the present text is really more about cultivating a relationship in which the preaching event will thrive than about offering some salient tips for survival at the pulpit. That we are all about relationship has been fairly ignored when it comes to developing preachers and good preaching in the long run. Preaching draws its power, not from rhetorical tricks, but from the spiritual momentum initiated by God in the call to preach in the first place.

This book is a roadmap to track the trajectory of the preacher: from the spirituality of call, through a relationship with the scriptures and the listeners, to an engagement with contemporary culture and media. It is both an affirmation and a challenge in the life and ministry of priests, deacons, and other ministers of the Word of God.

I guarantee you that this Seven-Step Ladder for Preaching will change the way you think about your next homily. I hope it helps affect the lives of countless parishioners who long to hear the saving Word—before we find the pews completely empty.

April 21, Feast of St. Anselm of Canterbury
Saint Meinrad, Indiana

Introduction

A CATHOLIC HOMILETIC?

The central claim of this book is that the liturgical homily embraces an essential process that is integral to the life and ministry of priests and deacons and to those they serve through the ministry of the Word of God. I am very much aware that there are any number of homily helps, workshops, and texts that suggest ways of improving Sunday preaching. These guides are useful tools. And yet, if the whole life of the preacher is not well integrated into the homiletic process, he will soon fall short of reaching the hearts, minds, and ears of the Christian assembly. The Sunday homily is not only the ten or so minutes that occur during the liturgy; it is the forum for Christian witness, the platform by which the minister of the Gospel interprets Scripture and Tradition in the context of Sacrament. The hope is that, in our preaching the Word of God, the liturgical assembly will hear of the marvelous deeds of the Lord accomplished in salvation history in language that is both graced and pastoral. For the Sunday homily to interpret Scripture within the lives of the congregation, preachers must reach to the very core of their relationship with the Lord, understanding their vocation to preach in the context of their own ministry and Christian service.

I have chosen the metaphor of a ladder to describe the homiletic process because of that image's strong biblical and ecclesial associations with evangelization. After Jacob left Beersheba for Haran, the Book of Genesis recounts that he fell asleep and had a dream about a ladder on which "angels of God were ascending and descending" (Gen 28:12). The Lord was revealed to Jacob standing beside him as the God of Abraham and his father Isaac. As a result of the dream, Jacob understands that the Divine Promise has been renewed, and he names the place *Bethel*, or "House of God."

The image of the ladder seems to be an appropriate way to rethink contemporary liturgical preaching since it is by way of ascending and descending a ladder that we envision the Lord, his House, and the faithful who come to worship in that dwelling place. Preaching must involve the renewal of the Divine Promise and a recollection of the salvation history that comes from marvelous, steadfast fidelity of the One who has called us into being. Remembering God's enduring love and promise makes the preacher the holder of sacred memory and the instrument of its faithful articulation in the liturgical assembly.

I am certainly not alone in using Jacob's Ladder as a dominant metaphor to discuss progress in a religious journey, or even preaching, for that matter. Perhaps most famously, Benedict of Nursia used the ladder to speak of the twelve steps of humility, and, in fact, it is often referred to as the Ladder of Humility. Later, St. Bernard of Clairvaux also echoed the idea of using a ladder to attain spiritual freedom and perfection. The Carthusian Guigo II spoke of a "Ladder of Monks" in a letter on the contemplative life. Alan of Lille's *The Art of Preaching* begins with an acknowledgment of Jacob's Ladder itself as a representation of the progress of a Catholic individual to perfection. Today, in a somewhat different context, 12-step programs are worldwide instruments for self-confrontation and maintenance of sobriety. Ladders represent process and progress toward integration; they are meant to take us from one world to the next, to lift us out of ourselves, paradoxically, after we have descended into the depths of understanding who we are as human beings, Christians, and ministers of the Gospel.

That said, the present volume is meant to be progressive, with each of the seven steps building on the previous ones. *Step One* is an invitation to see preaching in the wider context of a relationship between God and ordained ministry. I understand this initial step as a non-negotible entrance into the world of proclamation. The biblical witness makes clear that those called to bear the Good News do so after an encounter with the Holy. Therefore, preachers need to recognize that it is the reality of prayer and compassion for God's people that calls them into mission in the first place. Step One asks the homilist to consider his call and evolve a theology of preaching in light of a unique vocation.

Step Two draws from the interior understanding that the preacher has undertaken in the previous step and focuses his attention on the power of Word and Sacrament to gather the faithful. Facing a postmodern world of relativism and, sadly, meaninglessness, the preacher bears the sacred story of Christian redemption, which is contained not only in the Church's Lectionary, but in the *entirety and fullness* of Sacred Scripture. He preaches in the context of the Eucharistic Liturgy to offer a saving Word to those who hunger for meaning. Attending to the Church's doctrine becomes a way for the scriptures themselves to be actualized in the living faith community.

Step Three shifts the attention of the preacher more directly to those who hear in the Christian assembly. The preacher does not exist in a vacuum, but is called to mission for the sake of the People of God. As such, the hearer constitutes a fundamental reality in the homiletic act whose pastoral needs must be attended to by what the United States Catholic Bishops' exhortation on preaching, *Fulfilled in Your Hearing*, calls "naming grace." In what sense could a text be called a homily if these words have not been constructed with the hearer in mind? What are the essential elements that insure that the claims of the biblical texts on a given Sunday are actualized in the Christian assembly? How does the homily become a graced instrument so that the Good News is fulfilled in our hearing?

Step Four emerges directly out of the previous step and considers three methods that have been highly successful in framing homilies for hearers. David Buttrick has developed a method that grasps the intentionality of the scriptural text: What is the biblical reading doing? And, how can that be preached so that the consciousness of the hearer is altered by its proclamation? Eugene Lowry's narrative strategy deploys a technique that resembles the familiar plot structure of a Western. Lowry, like his mentor Fred Craddock, wants the biblical readings to be released like a cascade of living water on the congregation. The Christian community responds in an "aha" moment because the Gospel has come as both salvation and resolution. Lastly, Paul Scott Wilson constructs a method using four key elements of interrogation into both the scriptural text and the Christian community. Homiletic method explores the unfolding triumph of God's activity in human history, which the preacher and the congregation unpack together.

Step Five explores the way in which homiletic method is continually informed by contemporary communication theory. When it comes to understanding the way in which media has influenced how we deliver and receive messages in our culture, the preacher cannot afford to be passive. Along with method, a good homily has absorbed an understanding of recent rhetorical practices, particularly those in electronic media. Advertising and business communication methods should be investigated to see the ways in which listeners hear messages. As Church teaching has echoed for half a century, this step asks the preacher to form a real dialogue with culture for the sake of the Kingdom.

Step Six continues a dialogue with culture but also invites the preacher to begin to let go of prejudices that inhibit his encounter with the Word and the people for whom that Word has been sent. With a call to globalize the homily, the preacher must set aside the image he has of himself and begin to let the call to preach inform everything he does. This step takes the homilist out of the realm of method and into conversion, a process that was begun in Step One. The process continues in Step Six and again in Step Seven, becoming part of an interior discipline and self-inventory. What is the self-understanding that *I* bring to proclamation? Am I clinging to areas of "unfreedom" when it comes to serving the Word of God, including self-imposed identification of my own ministry? Have I really devoured God's Word in holy zeal, or have I held back part of my own ego for my own interests and appetites? The multicultural environment in the Catholic Church today is a test case for the preacher's authentic surrender and availability to the living Word.

Step Seven examines the potential pitfalls in preaching through the use of seven "case studies." This last step hazards an experience of self-confrontation that no good preacher can choose to ignore. There are lots of traps or just bad habits that face homilists as they minister the Word of God to the congregation. In addition to probing deep within themselves for traits of one or more of the preaching difficulties, perhaps the most significant way for homilists to improve and correct preaching on a significant level is through feedback from parishioners. True self-assessment will provide an instrument for understanding the homily that cannot be learned anywhere else because the listeners themselves are the guides to whether or not the Word has been heard.

These seven steps are ways to a more holistic homiletic, in my estimation, rooting the preacher in a consideration of prayerful reflection, pastoral urgency, scriptural and doctrinal teaching, and, finally, contemporary communication and homiletic methodology. At the same time, each step is made to stand on its own. Although this book is not comprised of "quick tips for better homilies," I have included some practical considerations in one way or another at the end of each section, together with some reflection questions. These queries are meant to induce homilists to ponder more deeply the step they have undertaken, as well as to prepare them for the next movement up the ladder.

Together with suggesting an integrative process of preaching—what I refer to as a Catholic homiletic—my intention in writing this book is also to provoke a discussion on the process of (ongoing) formation in Catholic homiletics. In the United States, the Catholic Church in the twentieth century made particular inroads in preaching and homiletic development, an event in cultural history that often goes unnoticed. As far as I can tell, the Catholic University of America, which established a national program for Catholic preaching, which ran from 1932 to 1960, was one of the only institutions to begin using audiotape feedback for teaching homiletics as early as the early 1930s. On a more popular level, when the *Catholic Hour* began on radio in 1930, it became an important and influential instrument of ecclesial and catechetical formation for millions of Catholics and other Christians throughout the country. The first speaker on the *Catholic Hour* was a young priest and professor of theology hailing from the Diocese of Peoria, Illinois, whose charisma, media savvy, and rhetorical skills eventually made him a primetime, preaching celebrity on both radio and then television: Fulton Sheen. Moreover, the laity had its part to play in evangelizing American culture as well. Largely responding to anti-Catholic sentiment at the time, "Evidence Guilds" sponsored lay street-preaching in the late 1920s and on into the next decades. Apologetic and catechetical preaching were practiced by women from Rosary College near Chicago and brought to missionary places like Oklahoma City. The Confraternity of Christian Doctrine would publish a manual of "street preaching" called *The Apostolate of Good Will* (1947). Lesser-known groups of laity—such as those that comprised the "Crusade for a More Fruitful Preaching" under the general sponsorship of the National Catholic Welfare Council/Conference—advocated better preaching during the Sunday liturgy. Religious orders, particularly the Dominicans, the Paulist Fathers, and the Society of Jesus, have also contributed countless resources in bearing the Good News to the People of God in the United States. In 1982, the USCCB published *Fulfilled in Your Hearing: The Homily in the Sunday Assembly*, still one of the best guides to the liturgical homily available.

Catholic preaching needs to be brought into an informed and lively discussion with twenty-first-century American culture. Much has changed since the publication of *Fulfilled in Your Hearing*: we now communicate through sound bites, collaborate more widely in ministry, and live in a multicultural, global environment. On February 25, 2008, the Pew Forum on Religion and Public Life released "U.S. Religious Landscape Survey," the results of its interviews with 35,000 adults. Forty-four percent of adult Americans now belong to a different church from the one in which they were raised. It seems that people change religions almost as often as they change jobs. Most Americans are more familiar with the eclectic images on YouTube than with the daily round of sermons or homilies in Christian worship. Stephen Prothero's data, demonstrated in his recent study *Religious Literacy* (2007), suggests that we are quickly becoming a nation of religious illiterates.

With generations of Catholics undercatechized and scripturally ignorant, what homiletic methods and tactics will make the Sunday homily an experience of deep faith and gratitude for the hearer? How can the Church's liturgy, sacred texts, and doctrine serve to build up the People of God through proclamation? What are the constitutive components that are part of Catholic homiletics?

My schema here is meant, finally, to gesture at what these homiletic elements might look like as a *process*, integrating the preacher, the text, and the assembly. Can seminaries and other theological formation programs begin to look seriously at a normative curriculum for homiletics that will prepare priests and permanent deacons to preach Christ and his Gospel for the contemporary parish?

I believe that the present time represents an exciting opportunity for Catholic preaching. Although ordained ministers and seminarians will find this book particularly useful in their ministry of the Word in preparing the liturgical homily for the Sunday Eucharist, lay ecclesial ministers who are more and more involved in a wide variety of preaching, from catechetics to apologetics, will find a lot of resources here as well. Moreover, although this book is primarily directed to Roman Catholic preachers, it is equally applicable to ecumenical circumstances. For reasons that should be obvious, the sharing in the Word of God establishes a graced and foundational commonality among the Christian churches.

As I write this, Pope Benedict XVI has just completed his historic visit to Washington and New York, a trip that brought good will, reconciliation, and the Gospel of peace. The Holy Father's call for a synod in October of 2008 on "The Word of God in the Life and Mission of the Church" has reminded us that the Word of God is living and active among us, something that he himself has shown the world by bringing Christ in faith, hope, and love to the United States. At the same time, the whole Church has been entrusted with the Sacred Scriptures for the sake of mission: we are nourished by the Word in order to be servants of the Word. And so those who are ordained ministers are challenged daily to renew their own calling to preach. The People of God await a new evangelization, but that renewal will happen only if those called to proclamation in the Christian liturgical assembly are themselves reconverted to the risen Christ, who sends us forth with the peace and joy of the Holy Spirit to all those with ears to hear the Good News.

April 21, Feast of St. Anselm of Canterbury
Saint Meinrad, Indiana

Step One

DISCOVERING A PERSONAL THEOLOGY OF PREACHING

Our homilies must be set aflame...a conversion that turns the preacher inside out.[1]

—Walter Burghardt, SJ

In chapter 7 of his *Rule for Monks*, St. Benedict describes the first step in his design for the Ladder of Humility as "vigilance to God's presence at all times and in all places." Acknowledging the presence of the Holy in everyday life, the monk is to remember that "he is seen by God in heaven, that his actions everywhere are in God's sight and are reported by angels at every hour." Similarly with preachers, our first step is an encounter with the God who calls us out of darkness into his own glorious light. It is a graced invitation that awaits our response.

The First Step in the Ladder of Preaching could not be more foundational: it asks us to probe the depths of our calling to encounter and make present the Word of God to those who long for meaning, who desire that their faith be deepened, and who, like the disciples on the road to Emmaus, await the moment when the presence of Christ will be opened to them in the Word and in the breaking of the bread. For those in ordained ministry, we must recall that our first duty is to proclaim the Gospel, a mission explicitly given at the Rite of Ordination: "Therefore, making the Word the object of your continual reflection, always believe what you read, teach what you believe, carry out in your life what you teach."[2] Above all, the preacher is one who remembers in prayerful gratitude both the call he has been given and the Lord who invited him to sow the seed with faith, hope, and love.

BIBLICAL ROOTS, SCRIPTURAL MODELS

Preaching begins and ends with the gifted expression of God's saving power inside human language. All baptized Christians are called to deepen their relationship with the God who has made them "a new creation"; however, this primal step into a profound, intimate relationship with the Lord grants those who serve the Word the capacity to be radically open to formation and conversion. Being aware of God's action in my life and in the world around me is the enticement into a lifelong relationship with the Holy. St. Augustine wisely advises the preacher that "at the very moment he steps up to speak, before he even opens his mouth and says a word, let him lift up his thirsty soul to God..."[3] But over the long term and in a variety of places, all good preachers must be enkindled in a prayerful discovery of God's saving work within the contours of a gifted existence. The preacher who is on fire with the Word of God gathers the various strands of life into a holocaust of desire. Preaching begins and ends with Holy Fire. There is a famous statement attributed to John Wesley who was once asked about the source of his effective preaching. Wesley said about his sermons, "I set my self on fire and the people come to watch me burn."

That fire has its origins at the edges of biblical history, in Moses' seminal encounter with God, as recorded in the Book of Exodus:

> Moses was keeping the flock of his father-in-law Jethro, the priest of Midian; he led his flock beyond the wilderness, and came to Horeb, the mountain of

God. There the angel of the LORD appeared to him in a flame of fire out of a bush; he looked, and the bush was blazing, yet it was not consumed. Then Moses said, "I must turn aside and look at this great sight, and see why the bush is not burned up." When the LORD saw that he had turned aside to see, God called to him out of the bush, "Moses, Moses!" And he said, "Here I am." Then he said, "Come no closer! Remove the sandals from your feet, for the place on which you are standing is holy ground."...

Then the LORD said, "I have observed the misery of my people who are in Egypt. I have heard their cry on account of their taskmasters....So come, I will send you to Pharaoh to bring my people, the Israelites, out of Egypt." But Moses said to God, "Who am I that I should go to Pharaoh, and bring my people, the Israelites, out of Egypt?" He said, "I will be with you; and this shall be the sign for you that it is I who sent you: when you have brought the people out of Egypt, you shall worship God on this mountain." (Exod 3:1–5, 7,10–12)

Moses' evocative, transformative encounter with God marks a moment of stepping into the wholly Other, the transcendent power that Rudolf Otto referred to in *Das Heilige* (1917) as *mysterium tremendum et fascinans*: a "tremendous and fascinating mystery." Moses was deeply attracted to the burning bush and faced an awesome God who drew this rough herdsman into a relationship with himself; God then required that the outlaw from Egypt remove his sandals while in the sacred place. Moses stands before Almighty God without his sandals, reminding us that the first step of those who are called to the ministry of preaching asks us to let go of our protective mechanisms and defenses. We stand before the Infinite God without our usual armor, waiting upon the Word. At the same time, this God hears the cry of a people in misery and urges Moses to liberation and mission. The fire of God burns for the sake of the human family and asks others to do the same. The divine promise given to a reluctant Moses is, "Now go, and I will be with your mouth and teach you what you are to speak" (4:12).

Like Amos after him, Moses was a herdsman-turned-prophet, plucked from obscurity in order to deliver the Word to a people longing to hear God's saving action in the course of human history. Indeed, the great prophets of Israel receive the Word after a seminal convergence with God. Jeremiah reckoned his prophetic commission from his youth and was spurred on after the Lord put out his hand and touched his mouth (Jer 1:9). After an overwhelming vision of God, Isaiah was called in the Jerusalem Temple. One of the heavenly seraphim in that beatific spectacle then touched his lips with a live coal taken from the altar. After experiencing the merciful God's profound forgiveness, the prophet said: "Here I am; send me!" (Isa 8). Having touched the loving presence of God's Word, the prophets are emboldened to take that Word to others. Ezekiel literally devoured the Word of God before his commission to preach: "He said to me, O mortal, eat what is offered to you; eat this scroll, and go, speak to the house of Israel" (Ezek 3:1). Ezekiel's ecstatic vision became a prophecy for his fellow exiles, bringing the message of hope and reconciliation. Ezekiel's consummation of God's message finds an echo in the Book of Revelation, where John was given a little scroll to eat. Like Moses, John's meeting with God is a strange mixture of sweetness and bitterness. God's Word is a delight to the mouth, but the fearful presence and judgment of the transcendent Holy One endures. John offers the Church a dynamic, apocalyptic vision of God's future, the triumph of the Lamb. The prophetic call to preach emerges from a source beyond the reckoning of the one who hears that voice: *Mysterium tremendum et fascinans.* As the apostle Paul understands his own vocation, the commission to preach the Gospel is the power of the cross, because "God decided, through the foolishness of our proclamation, to save those who believe. For Jews demand signs and Greeks desire wisdom, but we proclaim Christ crucified, a stumbling block to Jews and foolishness to Gentiles, but to those who are the called, both Jews and Greeks, Christ the power of God and wisdom of God" (1 Cor 1:21–24).

The wisdom of countless Christian preachers over the ages has informed us that there is no substitute for a personal relationship with God; this companionship becomes the fiery furnace that enables the spark of the sacred Word to take hold at the depths of our being. Moses admits to being slow of speech, yet he moved both Pharaoh and an entire people. As John of the Cross reminds us in the *Ascent of Mount Carmel*, when he discusses the preacher,

> No matter how lofty the doctrine preached, or polished the rhetoric, or sublime the style in which the preaching is clothed, the profit does not ordinarily increase because of these means in themselves; it comes from the spirit. God's word is indeed efficacious of itself according to David, who says that God will give to his voice the voice of power [Ps 68:33]; yet fire also has power to burn but will not burn if the material is unprepared.[4]

Taken together, these well-known biblical moments are luminous episodes of religious experience in which God's initiative provokes the one who receives the Word into prophetic utterance. God's Word is devoured and the preacher sets forth into mission. The definitive coming of the Word in Christ, though, represents a complete and definitive convergence of God's saving language in humanity. The Word became flesh and dwelt among us: the Incarnation makes visible the God we cannot see and reveals to us the trinitarian God through the work of Jesus' passion, death, and resurrection. While present in human history, Christ unfolded the Word, his very self, in the presence of his disciples:

> When he came to Nazareth, where he had been brought up, he went to the synagogue on the sabbath day, as

was his custom. He stood up to read, and the scroll of the prophet Isaiah was given to him. He unrolled the scroll and found the place where it was written: "The Spirit of the Lord is upon me,/because he has anointed me to bring good news to the poor./He has sent me to proclaim release to the captives/and recovery of sight to the blind,/to let the oppressed go free,/to proclaim the year of the Lord's favor." And he rolled up the scroll, gave it back to the attendant, and sat down. The eyes of all in the synagogue were fixed on him. Then he began to say to them, "Today this scripture has been fulfilled in your hearing." (Luke 4:16–21)

Jesus' explication of the Isaiah text reaches back to the ancient practice of preaching in Israel. In the Book of Nehemiah, Ezra stands before the assembly and "they read from the book, from the law of God, with interpretation. They gave the sense, so that the people understood the reading" (Neh 8:8). But more than a teaching, Jesus' interpretation of the Book of Isaiah is an incarnational moment, the living Word turned loose among those gathered to hear the Word proclaimed. Jesus is signaling an apocalyptic moment by his very presence among those who hear the Word. The Word is fulfilled in their hearing precisely because the Word himself has been definitively made known in a specific place and time in human history. As Pope Benedict XVI says in another context, "Jesus' teaching is not the product of human learning, of whatever kind. It originates from immediate contact with the Father, from 'face-to-face' dialogue—from the vision of the one who rests close to the Father's heart. It is the Son's word."[5]

Therefore, the passage in Luke 4:16–21 contains the blueprint for christological preaching: the gifted discovery of God's saving work within human language. Christ's witness at the synagogue in Nazareth is a fusion of the message proclaimed, the one who preaches the Word, and those who hear it in its fullness. In his proclamation of the Word, which is his very self, Jesus makes God present for those who will hear the Word of freedom and liberation he has come to proclaim.

The Incarnate Word becomes fulfilled in our hearing when our ears are radically open. The role of the assembly, then, forms a crucial and irresistible link with the preacher and the Word. And so the preacher's spirituality and theology of preaching must be rooted in the Word made visible in the People of God. The preacher becomes the first among the hearers, the representative of the community who is blessed because he hears the word of God and keeps it. The preacher is, above all else, a listener to the Word in the midst of the Christian assembly.

That experience of listening to God's self-communication in Christ takes us well beyond the confines of Nazareth and into the path of Jesus' other preaching as well. It was not for nothing that Jesus told the parable of the Sower and the Seed in Mark 4:1–20; the parable recalls the necessary position of the hearer as a partner in the preaching event. The Sower scatters his seed and it falls on the path, or on shallow ground, or on thorns, or, finally, on rich soil. Interpreting the parable allegorically, Jesus tells his disciples that the condition of the soil represents the conditions of listening. Those who receive the Word on shallow ground are foiled fairly quickly by distractions from the Evil One. Those on rocky soil hold on to the Word with joy only briefly; because they have no roots, tribulations foil their endurance. The seed that is sown among thorns are those who hear the Word but are choked by worldliness. Rich soil is emblematic of the listener in whose hearing the Word is fulfilled—yielding thirty, sixty, and a hundredfold. Jesus reminds his disciples of the vital, graced conditions that must be present to receive the Word with joy and bear fruit: the seed of the Word, the sower who scatters that Word, and the hearer of the Word who receives it with joy.

PRAYERFUL ATTENTION TO THE HEARER

The biblical and christological testimonies, briefly stated above, suggest that if we are to develop a mature spirituality of preaching, this life of prayer must be rooted in the Word of God and a love for God's people. The spirituality of preaching must find its ultimate strength from the twin fountains of contemplation and pastoral care. Personal prayer enlivens and sustains a God we have come to know. Care for God's people keeps us ever mindful of our mission to serve and of those to whom the Good News has been sent. Obviously, coming to terms with a personal spirituality of preaching does not mean a privatized and isolated vision of the homily. Every authentic spirituality of preaching will root us in a context, a cultural nexus, a profound recognition that the Kingdom of God is disclosed among the people who long for a saving word. When Moses encountered God in the desert, he did not linger in contemplation but was sent on mission. The preacher's formation does not occur in isolation but in the context of community. God drew Moses into relationship— sometimes a very painful one—for the sake of transformation through proclamation. Throughout the Book of Exodus we encounter a Moses who is an interpreter, a mediator between God and the community he serves.

In a homily preached when he was a deacon, one of my former students at Saint Meinrad recalled Moses' encounter with God in the Book of Exodus. Fr. Elkin Gonzalez Perez reminded us of the experience of the well-known Jesuit theologian and scientist Teilhard de Chardin, while on his way to China. Passing through the Suez Canal, he was struck by the two sides of ancient Egypt: one was a symbol of slavery, the other a theophany on Mount Horeb. Teilhard wondered if the bush was still burning. God made him realize that it *is* still burning, but not in Mount Horeb. The bush is burning in those who have God in their hearts and who try to make his presence known to the oppressed and hopeless.

It would be difficult to imagine a theology or spirituality of preaching that does not include a profound urgency to make the Word visible and active in God's people. Jesus' promise in Nazareth is a fulfillment in the hearing of those who will be set free. Graced preaching, then, claims the ears of the baptized so that Christ is made manifest in the midst of the assembly. It is the mission of the Church to reach out in love to the world—to preach, teach, and sanctify in the name of Christ. The opening lines of the Second Vatican Council's *Pastoral Constitution on the Church in the Modern World* remain a stunning reminder that the Church exists for the sake of God's people. "The joys and hopes, the griefs and the anxieties of the men of this age, especially those who are poor or in any way afflicted, these too are the joys and hopes, the griefs and anxieties of the followers of Christ. Indeed, nothing genuinely human fails to raise an echo in their hearts."[6] Christian preaching exists for the sake of mission to God's people. Moreover, the very nature of liturgical preaching is necessarily linked to Christ's saving work on earth. As the *Constitution on the Sacred Liturgy* tells us:

> Just as Christ was sent by the Father, so also He sent the apostles, filled with the Holy Spirit. This he did so that, by preaching the gospel to every creature (cf. Mk. 16:15), they might proclaim that the son of God, by His death and resurrection, had freed us from the power of Satan (cf. Acts 26:18) and from death, and brought us into the kingdom of His Father. His purpose was also that they might exercise the work of salvation which they were proclaiming, by means of sacrifice and sacraments, around which the entire liturgical life revolves.[7]

A listener-centered spirituality of preaching recognizes the God-given mission to strengthen the faith of the assembly. "So faith comes from what is heard, and what is heard comes through the word of Christ," is the well-known Pauline dictum of the Letter to the Romans in 10:17. Down through the centuries, the Church has acknowledged the pastoral importance of the hearer in preaching, an overall attention to the deepening of faith, or what St. Benedict refers to in his Rule as "listening with the ears of the heart." Recognizing the importance of the gathered assembly underlies the very definition of preaching for the Church fathers. In his *Book of Pastoral Rule*, Gregory the Great says: "Therefore according to the quality of the hearers ought the discourse of teachers to be fashioned, so as to suit all and each for their several needs, and yet never deviate from the art of common edification."[8] Writing in the Middle Ages, Alan of Lille was clear about the importance of the assembly's identity as a group. "Preaching should be public because it must be delivered not to one, but to many," he says. "If it were given to a single man, it would not be preaching but teaching—for that is where the distinction lies between preaching, teaching, prophecy and public speaking."[9]

For Maximus the Confessor, the Word of God came not only once at the Incarnation, but was made manifest in the hearts of the believers who listened to the Word proclaimed and desired to be even more present to that Word. "The Word of God, born once in the flesh (such is his kindness and his goodness), is always willing to be born spiritually in those who desire him. In them he is born as an infant as he fashions himself in them by means of their virtues. He reveals himself to the extent that he knows someone is capable of receiving him."[10]

Based on Church tradition, we can claim that the goal of preaching is nothing less than the transformation of the baptized, the Christian assembly, whose faith longs for a Word from God in order to be sustained. The *Directory for the Life and Ministry of Priests* says that "the ministry of the Word cannot be abstracted or distanced from the life of the people; indeed, it must make direct reference to the meaning of the life of man, of each man, and, therefore, must have a role in the most pressing questions present in the human conscience."[11] The hearer, then, is the goal of preaching, and a spirituality of preaching cannot be separated from evangelism's proper end, which is the increase of faith among the baptized. Preaching with the hearer in mind becomes an inspired activity of awakening for both the preacher and the assembly.

How can we evolve a spirituality of preaching that is pastoral and mindful of God's people? Again, the *Directory for the Life and Ministry of Priests* is quite clear about the relationship between the vital connection to be taken from our personal prayer with the scriptures and the ministry of charity: "The awareness of one's own mission to proclaim the Gospel must always find concrete expression in pastoral activity. Thus the diverse situations and settings in which he carries out his ministry will be vivified in the light of the Word of God."[12] Drawing from Jesus' own allegorization about the ways in which the Word is scattered and sown, we can see that the Word of God will be disclosed in many Spirit-filled arenas of life. Our meditation on the Word of God becomes incarnate in the course of the day and is disseminated when we preach about God in Christ. Indeed, the Word that dwells richly in the preacher is made manifest in so many encounters in pastoral ministry and, in the work of charity. We see the Word made visible in the liturgy, the scriptures, the assembly, the sacraments—and in what poet Gerard Manley Hopkins calls the "ten thousand places" where Christ plays. How can we separate the Word of God from where the living God has chosen to take up his home—hospitals, catechetical classes, the poor on the street, the lonely, and the forgotten? As Blessed Mother Teresa of Calcutta reminds the Church,

> The word of God becomes flesh during the day, during meditation, during Holy Communion, during contemplation, during adoration, during silence. That Word in you, you give to others. It is necessary that the Word live in you, that you understand the Word, that you love the Word, that you live in the Word. You will not be able to live that word unless you give it to others.[13]

We should stop at nothing to make Christ present in the Word and present in the preaching event. Motivating the Christian assembly, within the context of wherever they might find themselves on a particular day, becomes the ultimate challenge of preaching. John Henry Cardinal Newman calls this pastoral concern for the hearer the "one thing necessary" in preaching:

> I would lay down a precept, which I trust is not extravagant, when allowance is made for the preciseness and the point which are unavoidable in all categorical statements upon matters of conduct. It is, that preachers should neglect everything whatever besides devotion to their one object, and earnestness in pursuing it, till they in some good measure attain to these requisites. Talent, logic, learning, words, manner, voice, action, all are required for the perfection of a preacher; but "one thing is necessary"—an intense perception and appreciation of the end for which he preaches, and that is, to be the minister of some definite spiritual good to those who hear him. Who could wish to be more eloquent, more powerful, more successful than the Teacher of the Nations? Yet who more earnest, who more natural, who more unstudied, who more self-forgetful than he?[14]

That the preacher should be "self-forgetful" may strike us as something of an odd claim in an era of entertainment, but if Christ is to be taken as the paradigm for the preacher, then the focal point of our prayerful encounter with the Word of God will always be *other-centered*. Newman makes the shrewd point that the spirituality of the preacher is a grace resulting from the charity rendered to the care of those who hear. The interior growth in spirituality in preaching occurs to the extent that the preacher sacrifices his own self-cultivation for the sake of the congregation.

> I do not mean that a preacher must aim at *earnestness*, but that he must aim at his object, which is to do some spiritual good to his hearers, and which will at once *make* him earnest....It is this earnestness, in the super-

natural order, which is the eloquence of the saints, and not of saints only, but of all Christian preachers, according to the measure of their faith and love.[15]

The transformation of the preacher occurs, then, not by his own design but through his impulse to do spiritual good for the hearers. Newman uses the example of a man who has to cross a narrow abyss with a narrow plank. He accomplishes this passage not by looking at the board, but by keeping his eye on the object ahead of him. "To sit down to compose for the pulpit with a resolution to be eloquent is one impediment to persuasion; but to be determined to be earnest is absolutely fatal to it."[16]

Newman's perceptive observations about the crucial place of the hearer to the life of preaching would be echoed in the renewal of the Second Vatican Council. As is well known, *Gaudium et Spes* in particular placed special emphasis on the way in which the Gospel was enculturated, enfleshed in a dialogue with the world, making God's Word present in the context of the ages of humanity. As we have seen, the revelation of the Word of God has never been made in a vacuum, but always revealed, like Christ himself, inside human space and time.

> From the beginning of her history, [the Church] has learned to express the message of Christ with the help of the ideas and terminology of various peoples, and has tried to clarify it with the wisdom of philosophers, too. Her purpose has been to adapt the gospel to the grasp of all as well as to the needs of the learned, insofar as such was appropriate. Indeed, this accommodated preaching of the revealed Word ought to remain the law of all evangelization. For thus each nation develops the ability to express Christ's message in its own way.[17]

When seen in the light of the reforms of Vatican II, preaching is an invitation to re-present the Gospel in a new, grace-filled way—always in the context of where men and women work and love. God's self-communication is given a new hearing. *Sacrosanctum Concilium* reclaimed the long tradition of recognizing the assembly—together with the minister, the Word, and the sacramental elements—as a manifestation of Christ himself in the Eucharistic Liturgy.[18] Unified in gesture, the reception of God's Word would gather the baptized, strengthening their mystical relationship as the Body of Christ. Therefore the homily is to be seen as "part of the liturgy itself" and, as we are reminded in the *General Instruction on the Roman Missal* (2002), addressed to "the particular needs of the listeners." Moreover, echoing these liturgical instructions, the guidelines contained in *Presbyterorum ordinis* tell those ordained ministers who preach to be attentive to the hearers: "No doubt, priestly preaching is often very difficult in the circumstances of the modern world. If it is to influence the mind of the listener more fruitfully, such preaching must not present God's Word in a general and abstract fashion only but it must apply the perennial truth of the gospel to the concrete circumstance of life."[19]

The best expression of a postconciliar ecclesial position on preaching is the much-underutilized document issued by the NCCB in 1982, *Fulfilled in Your Hearing*, which recognizes the importance of the assembly by making that body its first priority. The pastoral priority of the homily should be uppermost in the mind of the preacher. Through theological reflection, the preacher brings the fruits of his contemplation to others. As *Fulfilled in Your Hearing* puts it:

> Unless a preacher knows what a congregation needs, wants, or is able to hear, there is every possibility that the message offered in the homily will not meet the needs of the people who hear it. To say this is by no means to imply that preachers are only to preach what their congregations want to hear. Only when preachers know what their congregations want to hear will they be able to communicate what a congre-

gation needs to hear. Homilists may indeed preach on what they understand to be the real issues, but if they are not in touch with what the people think are the real issues, they will very likely be misunderstood or not heard at all.[20]

Recognizing that *The Dogmatic Constitution on the Church* compels us to see the Church as "the mystery of God's saving will, given concrete historical expression in the people with whom he has entered into a covenant," *FIYH* calls the preacher to function as a "mediator of meaning" for this pilgrim people, by naming both grace and demons in the world.[21] Indeed, *FIYH* calls upon the preacher to be above all a person of prayer, and to listen to the word of God together with the assembly. "There is nothing more essential than prayerful listening for effective preaching, a praying over the texts which seeks the light and fire of the Holy Spirit to kindle the *now* meaning in our hearts."[22]

The role of *mediator* in the preaching event suggests that the preacher must heed the crucial integration between personal spirituality and what Fr. Ron Knott and others have called "spiritual leadership," the "ability of one person to influence others, through invitation, persuasion and example, to move from where they are to where God wants them to be."[23] To this end, Knott identifies homiletics, together with the presider's chair and the leadership role given to him for the faith community, as one of the key platforms in a triadic relationship in spiritual leadership. Coming to a well-informed theology of preaching allows the ordained minister to integrate the Church's mission with his own vocation. Homilists carry on the work of Christ's own work on earth when they preach through the gift of the Spirit. At the same time, maintaining a theology of preaching that is centered on the transcendent God and focused on mission is at the basis of the spiritual life. As Thomas Merton reminds us: "One of the paradoxes of the mystical life is this: that a man cannot enter into the deepest center of himself and pass through that center into God, unless he is able to pass entirely out of himself and empty himself and give himself to other people in the purity of a selfless love."[24]

PRACTICAL CONSIDERATIONS IN DEVELOPING A SPIRITUALITY OF PREACHING

✔ Discover biblical models of preaching in personal prayer.

If we are searching for a way to evolve a spirituality of preaching, then our first resource will be Sacred Scripture. I have already suggested the iconic status of Moses and the theophany at Mount Horeb as a window into the spirituality of the preacher. The destiny of Moses would be linked to the fate of the Word of God; that is, to his becoming the mediator of the Law in the desert for the people of Israel. What is the legacy of the Word of God from others in the Hebrew Scriptures? The prophets, the wisdom figures, great and small, all have their role to play. These characters and the process of their call to the service of the Word of God are marvelous models for preachers to discover in prayer.

In the New Testament, John the Baptist claims our attention as the linchpin fixed between two worlds, the old and the new covenants. The Book of Acts is also emblematic for a proper understanding of preaching in the early Church. St. Stephen the Protomartyr was murdered in the act of reinterpreting salvation history; that is, when he was preaching. We might recall this New Testament reality whenever there is a tough message that must be delivered to the congregation. Indeed, contemporary homilists can find an important theology and spirituality for their own pastoral ministry by encountering the way in which the early Christian community was transformed by the Word of God. Certainly, the Word himself, Christ Jesus, is the paramount example of how we ought to preach. Luke's description of Jesus at the synagogue has set in motion a way of understanding Christian preaching, but the parables also motivate us to understand preaching as life-changing moments of understanding the Word of God in the immediate historical context of everyday life.

Preachers evolve a spirituality of preaching through a devotional life as well. As Mother of the Incarnate One, Mary holds a position in the Gospel that suggests the way in which the Word has come to dwell in our midst. A profitable meditation is a reflection on Mary's encounter with the Word as it has come to be known in the Joyful Mysteries of the Rosary.

- *The Annunciation*: Mary is radically open to receiving the message of the Word of God from the angel Gabriel and consents to cooperate with God's plan.

- *The Visitation*: Having received the Word, Mary moves out to spread the news, first to her inner circle of family and friends. The baby who will become John the Baptist rejoices, even in the womb, at the presence of the Word, suggesting the powerful effect that the Good News has already had on one who is to preach that Gospel.

- *The Nativity*: The Word is made flesh as the angels and then the shepherds become sharers in the mystery of God made visible. The Word cannot keep silent, and so he is made known by both angelic choirs and simple herdsmen, the first to preach the Good News.

- *The Presentation*: The Word has come to be received by his own people under the Law of Moses. The Word encounters the Law, as the prophet receives the Incarnate One. Mary has given over God's Word to the tradition of Israel, where he is embraced by Simeon.

- *The Finding of the Word in the Temple*: The Word has been turned loose among the People of God, as Jesus discusses the Law with the elders in the Temple. Mary's dismay at losing sight of Jesus suggests that the Word is no longer hers, but the world's. The Word is already transforming those around him.

✔ **Consider the vital difference between private meditation and public efforts to draw others to live the Gospel, and work to bring these two worlds together.**

We are all called to holiness. Some evangelize with words; others do so more effectively by their actions. While all Christian people are called to respond to the gift of baptism through an ongoing personal relationship with the Christ that dwells within them, not everyone is called to preach. But to engage in the *ordained* ministry of preaching suggests that we have been called to transform the Christian assembly with whom we are partners, co-listeners to God's Word. Spiritual leadership is essential for proclaiming the Word. Personal piety, then, needs to be integrated into the vocation of Christian leadership and the sanctification of God's people.

The call to ordained ministry is modeled on Jesus, who spent the night in prayer before he engaged in his important ministry of choosing disciples, preaching, and healing. Indeed, the images that Jesus chose to express our commitment to transform the people through God's grace are instructive: The good shepherd leaves the ninety-nine sheep in search of the lost sheep. A man sells everything for a treasure hidden in a field. The merchant goes in search of a fine pearl of great price. Over and over again, Jesus reminds his disciples that we are called to holiness and to bring others to the same. Like Moses, the preacher sees the bright fire of a destiny infinitely larger than himself. To this end, there needs to be a private and personal experience of God that flows into the call to lead the people into the Promised Land that God has revealed. We arise from our contemplation as a stream moving from a great river, running for the sake of the Church, the People of God.

Needless to say, it should always be a crucial point of preaching preparation, then, to remember to be an *exegete for the assembly*. Those of us who were professionally trained as Christian ministers spent countless hours learning how to understand biblical texts through an important exegetical process.

That engagement with the Bible is necessary and fundamental in homily preparation. But there is another exegetical question about the *living text of the congregation*: Where have the faithful been over the past week? Have they received bad economic news? Has there been a significant news event or disaster in the area, which has played an important role in shaping the lives of the assembly? It would seem like common sense for preachers to meet people wherever they are, but this is not always the case. There are any number of disagreeable stories that could be told about the weekend following the devastation at the Pentagon and the World Trade Center on September 11, 2001. We know that some fundamentalists attributed this tragedy to God's revenge on what they judge to be America's lack of a moral backbone. These hypocritical judgments not withstanding, there were far more churches of every denomination who did not even acknowledge that the Tuesday before had been in any way different. That was a fatal flaw in preaching to the Christian assembly. Undoubtedly, members of the frightened congregation attending worship the weekend following 9/11 had images burned in their head: of people jumping off the Twin Towers, or the smoke and the rubble at Ground Zero flooding the streets of lower Manhattan, of people in despair and confusion.

Everyone going to a worship service on Sunday, September 16, 2001, had a huge question on their lips: Why? That question, spoken or unspoken by the congregation, still begs to be addressed by preaching that is pastoral and theological. What can Scripture reveal to the People of God in the face of such a tragedy? We face difficult questions of faith and life, some of which challenge our fidelity to the Lord. Like the Israelites wandering the desert and looking for hope from Moses, the Christian assembly searches for meaning in the overwhelming mystery of God. The ongoing relationship between God and his people is sustained by Word and Sacrament, mediated in the Christian assembly. There, the People of God encounter the love that will set them free, a Word that brings salvation.

✔ *Keep a Prayer-Homily Journal.*

A prayer-homily journal does not have to be a literary masterpiece, just a series of notes detailing the preacher's encounter with the sacred texts and what has occurred in the course of the week to inform them. I tell my students that they should begin to look at the Lectionary texts for the following Sunday early—preferably on the Monday before these readings are to be preached. These texts can form the spine of my prayer for the week in daily meditation. At the same time, the course of the week and my interaction with parishioners will undoubtedly reflect my position on how I will interpret the passages. For example, if I am to preach on the Fifth Sunday of Lent, Cycle A, the readings focus our attention toward the mystery of Christ's own resurrection and the coming Easter. Ezekiel 37:12–14 speaks of the Lord opening the graves of his people, while Paul in Romans 8:8–11 articulates a theology of the resurrection based on God's faithfulness. Certainly the powerful raising of Lazarus (John 11:1–45) reminds us of God's power in Christ to transform what was dead into new life.

If these readings are prayed over all week, they will take on a new meaning for both the preacher and the assembly; that is especially true, for instance, if there has been a tragic accident involving a death in the parish in the course of the week. The journal will become a source of integration, a record of personal insights about the texts that have become real in the course of the week. The experience of bringing the biblical readings into the concrete, historical situation of life echoes what *Fulfilled in Your Hearing* refers to as "preaching *through* the scriptures," not simply "on" them. The scriptures become a lens through which we see the current events of our lives as moments of "naming grace." If the goal of Sunday preaching is to bring the Christian assembly into a moment where they can acknowledge that the promise of God has been fulfilled in their hearing, then preaching through the scriptures ought to be the underlying mechanism preceding every preaching event. How do these scriptures give new meaning to our world today, right now? How does God's healing Word offer comfort to a congregation that may be unable to see the rich fare that has been offered to them in Word and Sacrament? The preacher is there, beckoned into being by the living God, to stand before the people and offer them a Word of salvation.

MISSTEPS

✕ *Ignoring the foundational relationship with God's Word.*

Failing to catch sight of God's burning love for us as it is revealed in Holy Scripture and the world around us is certainly not unusual. History is filled with folks who miss the sight of the Holy when God is disclosed in mystery. Such revelations may not be as dramatic as the theophany to Moses, but they are moments of grace waiting to be discovered. In her epic poem *Aurora Leigh*, Elizabeth Barrett Browning wrote—

Earth's crammed with heaven,
And every common bush afire with God;
But only he who sees, takes off his shoes.
The rest sit round it and pluck blackberries.[25]

Setting aside our daily concerns, whether they be tending sheep in the desert or fixing a broken boiler, is the first response in a call to a relationship with God in prayer. Fr. Hilary Ottensmeyer, a monk of St. Meinrad Archabbey, used to tell priests on retreat with him that "until you are convinced that prayer is the best use of your time, you will not have time for prayer." Drawn to the God who loves us with a love beyond all telling, we must turn aside to glimpse the manifestation of the Holy God.

✕ *Being unaware that this call to relationship with the Word is also an invitation to sanctify others in spiritual leadership.*

We might believe that our relationship with God is all about us. Nothing could be further from the truth. Our personal piety is necessary but it is not enough. Christ calls his disciples to bear witness and to bring the Gospel of peace and joy, justice and hope, and praise and thanksgiving to all. As I have suggested earlier in this chapter, this particular step has its roots deep in the biblical and ecclesial tradition. The motive to sanctify the Church is a mandate given at ordination, together with preaching and teaching. This call to mission in spiritual leadership for the sanctity of others requires first of all a profound respect for the dignity of the baptized assembly. Aloofness, a know-it-all attitude, or arrogant behavior is completely out of place for the preacher bringing the Word of God to rest in the presence of the congregation. Needless to say, an emphasis on personal piety to the detriment of the Christian assembly suggests a nightmare for the parish on many levels, and not all of them limited to homiletics. It is hard to imagine a "true" piety that is self-absorbed and dominated by ideological concerns being preached well from a graced pulpit.

An anonymous parishioner wrote an article in *America* magazine about her parish being broken by the coming of a new pastor. "He also believes that the parishioners are the sheep and he is the shepherd, which translates to: My way or the highway. He enjoys all the power, without the intuition or skill of leadership."[26] If the preacher does not remember that he is a co-listener with the baptized to the Word of God, then his spirituality will be self-serving and his preaching the result of what Newman calls self-conscious "earnestness." Obviously when we are speaking about a foundational relationship with the Word of God that is lacking, the theological and ecclesial issues that follow will be profound and even tragic. The First Step on the Ladder of Preaching requires that we meet God as the Holy Other—in word, in sacrament, in community, in personal prayer. We remain radically open to this God who comes to us in the desert of our longing. Preachers take off their sandals when choosing to encounter the Holy, turning aside from preoccupations to encounter the Word living among us.

QUESTIONS AND PROJECTS FOR CLASS

1. Ask each student to write a five-page paper on a personal theology of preaching, and then discuss their essays in class.

2. Have the students break into pairs. Give each pair one of the following questions: Why preach? What to preach? To whom are you preaching? How to preach?

3. Ask a group of students to do a presentation to an imaginary RCIA class on the importance of the hearer in the liturgical assembly.

QUESTIONS FOR REFLECTION

1. What is my theology of preaching? How do I see myself in relation to the Christian liturgical assembly?

2. How has my ecclesiology influenced my theology of preaching? Do I see myself as an "interpreter of meaning" for the people I serve?

3. How can I foster a better prayer life for my life in Christ?

4. What can I do to listen more carefully to God and to the assembly?

Step Two

KNOWING THE POWER OF
THE BIBLE AND THE LITURGY

Your word is a lamp to my feet and a light to my path.
—Psalm 119:105

If liturgical preaching that is mindful of personal prayer and centered on the needs of the hearers is crucial for the First Step in the Ladder of Preaching, the question that faces us next is, "How?" How will the preacher gather together the People of God in prayer and Word? The answer should not surprise us when we hear the familiar lines from John's Gospel: "And I, when I am lifted up from the earth, will draw all people to myself" (John 12:32). Christ, lifted on high on the cross, himself becomes the center for all people, for all races and tongues. And so the Church is drawn by the power of the Holy Spirit into the saving power of Christ at the altar of Word and Sacrament, the place where the Lord is made present in the midst of the assembly. Scripture becomes the language of the story of salvation, a story that invites the community to recall together God's wonderful works, most especially the life, death, and resurrection of Jesus. At the same time, the Church's liturgy brings together those who are longing to be fed by the God who has offered himself up as a gift for all humanity, high on the cross. The homilist, then, preaches Christ crucified, lifting him up for all to see. In the

Second Step, it is pivotal, then, that the one who proclaims the Word is aware of the potency of Scripture and the liturgy to collect and shape the Christian assembly in Christ's name. Once again, the preacher finds the contours of his identity in the person of Christ himself: "And just as Moses lifted up the serpent in the wilderness, so must the Son of Man be lifted up, that whoever believes in him may have eternal life" (John 3:14–15).

SALVATION HISTORY AND THE CRISIS OF POSTMODERNISM

We are converted through story—God's story. The remembrance of God's wonderful deeds in the course of human history becomes the substance of Word and worship. As the psalm reminds us, "We ponder your steadfast love, O God, in the midst of your temple" (Ps 48:9). The readings from Scripture and the celebration of the liturgy draw the People of God into the presence of Christ, where his free gift to the Father, in the unity of the Holy Spirit, becomes "a living sacrifice of praise." The scriptures are not simply folk tales or myths from the past, but God's revelation in history expressed in sacred Word and symbol that continually form new faith communities. Paul tells Timothy: "Continue in what you have learned and firmly believed, knowing from whom you learned it, and how from childhood you have known the sacred writings that are able to instruct you for salvation through faith in Christ Jesus" (2 Tim 3:14–15). As *Dei Verbum* of the Second Vatican Council reminds us,

> The Church has always venerated the divine Scriptures just as she venerates the body of the Lord, since from the table of both the Word of God and of the body of Christ she unceasingly receives and offers to the faithful the bread of life, especially in the sacred liturgy. She has always regarded the Scriptures together with the sacred tradition as the supreme rule of faith, and will ever do so....Therefore, like the Christian religion

itself, all the preaching of the Church must be nourished and ruled by sacred Scripture. For in the sacred
books, the Father who is in heaven meets His children
with great love and speaks with them; and the force
and power of the word of God is so great that it
remains the support and energy of the Church, the
strength of faith for her sons, the food of the soul, the
pure and perennial source of spiritual life.[1]

Both scripture and the Church's liturgy recall, in mystery,
God's story of salvation, which the preacher reframes in grace
for the assembly. When the deacon Stephen preached against the
Temple in Acts 7:2–53, he rearticulated and reinterpreted the
Judaic story of salvation through the lens of Jesus' resurrection.
The protomartyr begins with Abraham and then recounts Joseph
and Moses, David and Solomon. Stephen accuses Israel's clerical
establishment of building God a house made of stone instead of
preparing for the Lord a holy tabernacle of their own lives.
Stephen's preaching is a prophetic indictment of the high priest
and other members of the Temple who opposed the Holy Spirit
and killed "the Righteous One." Therefore, if Stephen applies his
reading of the Hebrew Scriptures following the death and resurrection of Christ, the scriptural narrative of the past functions as
a witness to the living truth of the Gospel.

Through Christian biblical preaching, sacred *anamnesis*
transforms the community as the past speaks to the present in a
new way. Vatican II and *Fulfilled in Your Hearing* rightly emphasize that the homily is to be rooted in Scripture, recalling the
marvelous deeds of the Lord and his love. When *Dei Verbum* discusses the liturgical homily, it is in the context of a reflection on
all of Sacred Scripture. "By the same word of Scripture, the ministry of the word also takes wholesome nourishment and yields
fruits of holiness. This ministry includes pastoral preaching, catechetics, and all other Christian instruction, among which the
liturgical homily should have an exceptional place."[2] *Fulfilled in
Your Hearing* echoes the Council's observations, and the

preacher draws from Scripture to gather the Christian assembly, helping the community to interpret the "signs of the times."

> The Christian interprets the world not as a hostile and evil place, but as a creation of a loving God who did not allow it to destroy itself, but sent his Son to rescue it....
>
> The preacher then has a formidable task: to speak from the Scriptures (those inspired documents of our tradition that hand down to us the way the first believers interpreted the world) to a gathered congregation in such a way that those assembled will be able to worship God in spirit and truth, and then go forth to love and serve the Lord.[3]

Yet, despite the fundamental need to root the Word in the pastoral context of the lives of others, the preacher faces numerous obstacles. Increasingly, speaking the scriptures has become more and more difficult in preaching because of a culture of general biblical illiteracy and fragmentation. The age of technology has brought with it an interest in the visual, the instantaneous, the sound bite. With increasing multitasking as part of everyday life, even those who have a natural piety often find it difficult to absorb the narrative features of the ancient biblical text. Gallup polls indicate over and over again that there is a disappearance of even the most rudimentary knowledge of the Bible. The lack of religious and biblical vocabulary becomes more obvious in political campaigns, when a candidate such as Howard Dean can mistakenly identify the Book of Job as his favorite New Testament book, or when few folks seem to get the biblical allusions that former presidential candidate Mike Huckabee includes in his rhetoric. Stephen Prothero says that "according to recent polls, most American adults cannot name one of the four Gospels, and many high school seniors think that Sodom and Gomorrah were husband and wife." He goes on to say that the same folks who were able to name the four Beatles were incapable of recalling any of the twelve apostles.[4]

35

Complicating the problem of biblical and religious literacy is the phenomenon commonly referred to as postmodernism, which rejects the past or views it through irony or an ironic self-awareness. The result, in short, is that our culture faces a problem of coherence, even lack of meaning; this is a failure to grasp history, or even a grand "arch-story" of salvation. We have long known that we are a nation of "rugged individuals" who subscribe to individualism as if it were a religion. But now we live in a "virtual" world, meaning we can be alone with computer games, the Internet, the cell phone. The sense of common history and origins has become something that few people appreciate, and they often look at religion and its artifacts as something like a "museum culture." What does the story of salvation as it is proclaimed in the scriptures now mean to a culture that appears dislodged from history and lives in a frenetic present tense? How is the preacher now going to recapitulate the ongoing song of God's salvation in Christ to a congregation that has been cut off from its historical legacy as a Church? In certain ways, our world is composed of numerous ministories, lives that we watch on television or follow in the news, all of which briefly pass away to be taken up by other mininarratives. Consumerism encourages us to forget what we bought in the past and to live in the present.

Ours is a culture of forgetting, not remembering. In her brief but marvelously insightful book *Illness as Metaphor*, the late Susan Sontag unmasks the ways in which diseases have been appropriated by various cultural forms to mark the identity of a particular century. For example, tuberculosis, which was rampant in the nineteenth century and was marked by the complexities of the emerging Industrial Revolution, has come to influence the way we think of that period. For Sontag, the narratives of the nineteenth century were dominated by the memory of that particular disease and thus structure the way we think of that period. Following Sontag's metaphorical train of thought in broad strokes, we might one day come to think of the twenty-first century, not as a tubercular age with its diminishment of the body, but as an "Alzheimer's age," with its shrinkage of memory.

Postmodernity has signaled for us the age of Alzheimer's, or the era of forgetting, of misidentifying history.

For some early theorists of postmodernism, such as Robert Venturi and his colleagues, Las Vegas is the premier postmodern city. Why? Precisely because it is a city without a center, a seemingly endless design of pastiche and nostalgic architectural formations that do not recall the past so much as parody it. It is a city without a history. Postmodernity is irrevocably linked to a failure to remember the past, even while it craves nostalgia and pastiche; it forgets the reality of both the collective self and the individual self within history. To be in the midst of postmodernity is to live like the seemingly ubiquitous action hero Jason Bourne, on the edge of being a complete self, always fragmenting and searching for a past. The culture of postmodernism is episodic, where consumers are kept free from remembering in order that they can move on to the next purchase. Postmodernity is a supermarket culture full of endless choices and an ironic arena of struggles, with a dubious moral imagination and a mindset of shifting relativism.

Whether we acknowledge it or not, postmodernism has shaped those who hear the Word of God and invariably challenges the way in which we think about preaching as well. Despite the complexity in dealing with an issue that almost everyone has an opinion about (just use the word *postmodernism* and most people think you have had at least some continuing ed credit), I think we can meet the culture of fragmentation with Gospel optimism and faith in the Word living and dwelling among us. Ultimately, our preaching is about the Word made flesh, the historical reality that is part of salvation history. Our preaching extends beyond instant messaging, therapeutic promises, and an evacuation of history.

Philosopher Jean-François Lyotard described the culture of postmodernity as the disappearance of the "metanarrative." What he means by this we can probably guess. Lyotard says that there is no longer a grand narrative that binds the culture together; instead, we have become a tissue of millions of "micronarratives."

Here, we have only to recall Andy Warhol's celebrated observation that in the future, everyone will be famous for fifteen minutes. That is the real story now—literally a different narrative every night—when millions of viewers tune in to reality television shows (by far the most popular genre on TV), or see *Extreme Home Makeovers* or Dr. Phil or Oprah and their many different variations and mutations. These micronarratives play easily in a culture of individualism in which the sense of the collective or the common good has been dismissed outright like an unwanted guest. For years, the entertainment industry has been in the business of the theatrics of neurosis, seeing bits and pieces of people's lives, famous or not, paraded on the screen. The unity of the past, once the very fabric of the way in which one culture handed down its tradition to another, appears to be ruptured and lacks both a central narrative and those capable of retelling the story. William Butler Yeats gives us a glimpse of this apocalypse of narrative in his famous poem "The Second Coming," in which he writes of dissolution, anarchy, and the drowning of innocence in a tide dimmed by blood.

THE UNITY OF SCRIPTURE AS STORY

We could go on and on about cultural fragmentation, about which much theory has recently been generated by cultural critics. The point is that the preacher is going to have a formidable task: the homilist must advert to a concept of salvation history that is all about coherence, in a society in which, as Yeats put it, "the center cannot hold." The preacher must become the central storyteller in our culture, recapitulating salvation history in a liturgical setting. As *Fulfilled in Your Hearing* says,

> One of the most important and most specifically human ways in which faith is communicated to individuals and communities is through language. The way we speak about our world expresses the way we think about it and interpret it. One of the reasons we speak

about our world at all is to share our vision of the world with others. The preacher is a Christian specially charged with sharing the Christian vision of the world as the creation of a loving God.[5]

Indeed, the scriptures are an account of the faith community, in sacred story that is recalled and treasured in the Christian tradition. Consider the way in which Jesus transformed the disciples at Emmaus with the recounting of his interpretation of the scriptures. "Were not our hearts burning within us while he was talking to us on the road, while he was opening the scriptures to us?" (Luke 24: 32). The disclosure of the risen Lord in Word and Sacrament becomes the occasion for conversion and transformation from despair to hope, from fragmentation to wholeness. Jesus reframed the scriptures for the needs of his disciples traveling on the road to Emmaus. As Ronald Rolheiser reminds us, "To gather around the word of God and the breaking of the bread is a ritual gathering and ritual brings something that normal social gathering does not, namely, transformative power beyond what can be understood and explained through the physical, psychological, and social dynamics that are present."[6]

Most obviously, the liturgy itself harkens back to sacred memory, given to us when Christ was personally present here on earth. But from the perspective of the listener, we must begin to ask a tough question: How can we preach and sing of our salvation in Christ when even the foundation of knowledge in a divine plan for grace and redemption is placed in jeopardy by the loss of a metanarrative? This question of relativism is at the core of what the Church, and most recently Popes John Paul II and Benedict XVI, have consistently argued against, and with good reason. That the living God has entered into our history, suffered, died, and redeemed us; that we have come from a Judeo-Christian tradition and are a pilgrim people here on this earth; that we are destined for a heavenly city where we will one day, hopefully, see God face to face in the company of the blessed: these are all foundations, or ways of knowing, that thrive on cherished assumptions about the good, the true, and the beautiful, but which the disappearance of the grand story of our origin and destiny has placed in a state of forgetfulness.

The Christian community must recollect the story of salvation in its fullness, from Genesis to Revelation. *And this holy memory remains the special province of the preacher who is the keeper of sacred story. He is charged with keeping the story of salvation alive. Therefore, the sacred text of the Judeo-Christian tradition, the Bible, must be owned in its entirety.* If the preacher cannot claim the entire Bible as a source of inspiration and a foundational resource for prayer, he will be unable to persuade others to see the sacred text as a witness to God's revealed love to the world. Alan of Lille says,

> This should be the form of preaching: it should develop from, as it were, its own proper foundation, from a theological authority—especially a text from the Gospels, the Psalms, the Epistles of Paul, or the Books of Solomon, for in these, in particular, edifying instruction resounds. Texts should also be taken from other books of Holy Writ if necessary, and if they have a bearing on the theme at hand.[7]

Dei Verbum makes it very plain that without a nearness to the Word, preachers will soon run dry. Quoting St. Augustine, *Dei Verbum* says that "this cultivation of Scripture is required lest any of them become 'an empty preacher of the word of God outwardly, who is not a listener to it inwardly' since they must share the abundant wealth of the divine word with the faithful committed to them, especially in the sacred liturgy."[8] *Fulfilled in Your Hearing* advises getting "behind" the Scriptures, meditatively and prayerfully, asking, "What is the human situation to which these texts were originally addressed? To what human concerns and questions might these same texts have spoken through the Church's history? What is the human situation to which they can speak today?"[9] Here, we might recall how important Step One in the Ladder of Preaching is to supporting a foundation cultivated in Step Two: Prayerful familiarity with the sacred texts in our tradition recognizes the dynamic pattern in revelation and the healing power of the Word of God for his people. The "mediator of meaning" preaches from the horizon of human history and its interface with God's Word; that is the work of interpretation: naming grace in the world.

In 1993, the Pontifical Biblical Commission issued *The Interpretation of the Bible in the Church*, recommending the broadening of the spectrum of interpretation of the Bible. Cardinal Joseph Ratzinger (now Pope Benedict XVI) said in the preface,

> The text of the document inquires into how the meaning of Scripture might become known—this meaning in which the human word and God's word work together in the singularity of historical events and the eternity of the everlasting Word which is contemporary in every age. The biblical word comes from a real past. It comes not only from the past, however, but at the same time from the eternity of God and it leads us into God's eternity, but again along the way through time, to which the past, the present and the future belong.[10]

Recognizing an enormous range of interpretive options open to those reading scripture, *The Interpretation of the Bible in the Church* says that "within the one Christian Bible, the relationships that exist between the New and the Old Testaments are quite complex."[11] Being able to see the entire Bible through the hermeneutical lens of "re-readings" (*relectures*) is unique to the Bible itself, granting the text inner unity. Such re-readings "develop new aspects of meaning, sometimes quite different from the original sense. A text may also make explicit reference to older passages, whether it is to deepen their meaning or to make known their fulfillment."[12] For example, the promise made by

God to Abraham in Genesis 15:7, 18 becomes entrance into the sanctuary in Exodus 15:17, and then in Hebrews 3:7—4:11 it is "reserved for those who have faith," and finally fulfilled with "the eternal inheritance" of Hebrews 9:15.

The opportunities for intertextual interpretation for the preacher are seemingly limitless in reading the Bible. As is well known, St. Augustine, and other patristic writers such as Origen, developed intricate allegorical readings of the Old Testament as types of the New. To mention one of the most famous examples: The sacrifice of Abraham of his son Isaac foreshadowed the God who gave up his only son for the sake of our redemption. On the level of allegory, Isaac becomes a type of Christ. Drawing from the treasure of such interpretations, Pope Benedict has reminded the Church of the important dynamic that exists between the Old and New Testaments:

> The proper interplay of Old and New Testaments was and is constitutive for the Church. In his discourses after the Resurrection, Jesus insists that he can be understood only in the context of "the Law and the Prophets" and that his community can live only in this properly understood context....Today's widespread temptation to give the New Testament a purely spiritual interpretation, in isolation from any social and political relevance, tends in the same direction.[13]

The Interpretation of the Bible in the Church states that all these intertextual connections necessitate a reading of the entire scriptures in order to access multiple meanings, because "there is a mutual illumination and a progress that is dialectic: what becomes clear is that Scripture reveals the meaning of events and that events reveal the meaning of Scripture, that is, they require that certain aspects of the received interpretation be set aside and a new interpretation adopted." The document goes on to make its point by singling out naively literalist approaches (fundamentalism), suggesting that presenting nonbiblical ideological truths without taking into account a historical tradition "misrepresents the call voiced by the Gospel itself."[14] Preaching absorbs fundamentalist approaches when it lacks interpretation and simply isolates passages from the Lectionary as moral or religious dictums. The new *Sunday Lectionary* that was revised in 1969 to include a three-year cycle has been an enormous gift to the Church, but the drawback for preaching lies in a potential loss of textual context. My scripture professor at the seminary once likened the experience of reading the *Sunday Lectionary* week after week to a congregation reading index cards. These "slices" from the Bible are free-floating texts searching for a wider contextual reading. As preachers, then, we must see what Bernhard W. Anderson has called "the unfolding drama of the Bible."[15]

Some of these reframings of context for preaching are broad and others are more subtle. On the Third Sunday of Lent A, the Gospel is the story of the Samaritan woman at the well. It is a marvelous narrative, full of rich baptismal imagery and connections with the first reading from Exodus, in which God gives his people water from a rock. The Lectionary then begins its Gospel reading with John 4:5: "So he came to a Samaritan city called Sychar." But in the four verses before this passage we notice a complication concerning Jesus' motivation for the journey; its inclusion enriches the theological meaning of the story: "Now when Jesus learned that the Pharisees had heard, 'Jesus is making and baptizing more disciples than John'—although it was not Jesus himself but his disciples who baptized—he left Judea and started back to Galilee. But he had to go through Samaria." These verses function as a transition to the discourse of the Samaritan woman at the well. As Raymond Brown pointed out, "Jesus' departure from Judea seems to mean the end of his ministry of baptizing; henceforth his ministry will be one of word and sign."[16] My point is not that the *Sunday Lectionary* should have necessarily included this transitional passage but that its position in the scriptures is significant to a reading of antecedent and subsequent material. This background becomes an important piece for the preacher in understanding and interpreting the power of Jesus' encounter with the Samaritan woman: he is offering her a living sign of redemption—his very self as living water—a sign offered first to a woman of Samaria beyond his own people in Judea. There are numerous examples in the *Sunday Lectionary* that could illustrate the importance of filling in the *entirety* of scripture.

The challenge for the preacher remains to fill in what is lacking in such gaps, making the connections that need to be enunciated for the sake of the proclamation of the *whole* Gospel. Making connections from Sunday to Sunday also suggests a unity in the scriptures that remind us of the formative power of the Church's liturgy in using these specific texts. We weave together the Pauline epistles when they are aware of the Apostle's rhetorical strategy and theology. As Frank Matera explains, preachers "realize that, while they may not preach from Paul every week, there are periods of two or three weeks when it is opportune to employ the Pauline texts to develop themes such as faith, justification, resurrection, life in community, the power of the Spirit, etc. In other words, preachers need to plan their preaching and decide when and how to preach from Paul."[17] *Sacrosanctum Concilium* famously makes the point that the scriptures and their tradition ought to unfold before the People of God more expansively, saying that the "treasures of the Bible are to be opened up more lavishly, so that richer fare may be provided for the faithful at the table of God's Word." In asking for a three-year cycle of readings for the new Lectionary, the document asks then for a "more representative portion of the holy Scriptures" to be read for the faithful.[18]

Now the practical instruction stated in the Council document was the revision of the Lectionary, but the implication to bring forth a "richer fare" remains clear for a broader dissemination of understanding: that a widening of the horizon of Scripture will nourish God's people. Undoubtedly, the plethora of images and symbols in Scripture has provided listeners common ground for centuries and has worked to gather the hearers at the table of the Word and beyond. Consider, for instance, the way the Book of Exodus was read as a discourse to lead African Americans out of slavery and into freedom. "The Promised Land" was repositioned as a place where equality and civil rights would be expected. Dr. Martin Luther King preached as a kind of new Moses, leading an entire generation into a new vision of moral justice. Biblical imagery and the metaphorical structures of scripture give the preacher a language, a universal story, for the listener. The preacher, then, provides a new, invigorating narrative for the Christian assembly, enabling the faithful to claim their role as those who hear the Word of God anew.

> Searching out biblical imagery merges with the task of considering the adequacy of the symbolism we use to express the truth of relationships—social, institutional, and personal. What does the Bible tell us about the city as an expression of the reign of God? What does a city look like that does not do violence to the created nature of its male and female citizens? The church is called the Body of Christ. What does it mean to express the wholeness of the body in our ecclesiastical structures? In the many masculine and feminine images which describe God and God's activity, what do we learn about human parenthood, about the relationships between coworkers, between lovers, between brothers and sisters?[19]

Preachers ought not to underestimate the power of language and symbol to shape a congregation. The Book of Acts records that when the early Church faced persecution in Jerusalem, the disciples were scattered throughout the countryside of Judea and Samaria.

> Now those who were scattered went from place to place, proclaiming the word. Philip went down to the city of Samaria and proclaimed the Messiah to them. The crowds with one accord listened eagerly to what

was said by Philip, hearing and seeing the signs that he
did, for unclean spirits, crying with loud shrieks, came
out of many who were possessed; and many others
who were paralyzed or lame were cured. So there was
great joy in that city. (Acts 8:4–8)

Anyone who has even a cursory acquaintance with rhetoric
knows that what we say has the ability to change others. In the
world of advertising, a clever caption or image will boost product sales exponentially. "Obey your thirst!" was a very successful slogan for Sprite that told people to "trust your gut." That
caption suggests a shift in priorities: buying a soft drink is not a
casual purchase, but something like an intuitive command from
deep within the self. Language tells us how to behave.

So the Church is charged with leading the faithful into a
banquet made up of a "richer fare." Providing metaphors that
challenge our worldview, biblical preaching confronts the dominant culture's prevailing status quo attitude. Clearly, Jesus' parables were reorienting his own hearers into "Kingdom language."
Consider, for instance, how referring to the Kingdom of God as
a mustard seed must have struck a pious Jewish layman from
the first century. As several scholars have pointed out, the
Kingdom of God might have been associated with power and
glory—perhaps like a cedar of Lebanon, long associated in the
Hebrew Scriptures with messianic might. But a tiny mustard
seed? How could Jesus possibly compare the Kingdom of God to
a mustard seed? "When sown upon the ground, [it] is the small-
est of all the seeds on the earth; yet when it is sown it grows up
and becomes the greatest of all shrubs, and puts forth large
branches, so that the birds of the air can make nests in its shade"
(Mark 4:30–32). This little parable chides us into a new way of
receiving God's power. Jesus' parabolic language provides his
hearers with an astonishing alternative to their status quo vision,
reorienting them from their present condition into God's future:
The Kingdom of God is like a tiny seed that grows because it has
been sown and cared for by preaching that Kingdom on earth;

there, it shelters and harbors God's children in its protective branches. In a certain sense, Jesus himself provides us with a kind of homiletic, a rationale for Kingdom language that must be sown in order for the Kingdom to be effective. When it is planted, the mustard seed of preaching yields a harvest of justice and protection in God's arms.

THE PREACHER AND THE COLLECTIVE IMAGINATION

The classical biblical parable operates as an ambiguous narrative, teasing us into a meaning we may not have expected. Scriptural language and symbol are so intensely rich that they often leave us with a superabundant meaning beyond our predispositions. As liturgy scholar Nathan Mitchell puts it, "Every symbol deals with a new discovery and every symbol is an open-ended action, not a closed-off object."[20] No less important for the homilist than preaching the whole Gospel is an attitude that recognizes the power of the liturgy—its language, its tradition, its great feasts. The integral relationship between Word and Sacrament cannot be emphasized enough as a foundation for liturgical celebration and preaching. The preacher makes connections between the language of scripture and our faith response in the celebration of the Eucharist. Indeed, it is precisely the preacher's purpose to facilitate a grateful Christian assembly toward a movement from Word to Sacrament. The language of the liturgy is the faithful lifting up of our hearts in thanksgiving for the outpouring of the love of the Son to the Father. Therefore, the liturgical texts themselves have their own part to play in the homily. In his revisiting *Fulfilled in Your Hearing*, Edward Foley challenged the document "to consider the 'liturgical Bible' as further including the ritual actions, and even the feasts and seasons that we celebrate throughout the year."[21]

Consider, for instance, this passage from an Advent Preface (Advent II) in the *Sacramentary*:

His future coming was proclaimed by all the prophets.

The virgin mother bore him in her womb with love beyond all telling.

John the Baptist was his herald and made him known when at last he came.

In his love, Christ has filled us with joy as we prepare to celebrate his birth, so that when he comes he may find us watching in prayer, our hearts filled with wonder and praise.

This language from the *Roman Missal* is filled with images and symbols that are ripe for preaching. The Preface moves along a kind of plot, announcing the coming of Christ from the prophets, through his mysterious virgin birth, to the present where Christ is still filling us with joy. We are also encouraged to think about the joy that overflows from the expectant celebration of the nativity to keeping faithful vigil for his coming. Here, then, we might consider preaching about the important ways in which the coming of Christ has been made known to us—in the flesh, in prayer, at the end-time. Indeed, the eschatological quality of Advent as an "almost but not yet" lurks at the edges of this Preface. Preaching on this text is a clear instance of gathering the community under the majestic roof of liturgical language, artful expressions that rehearse the story of salvation; it asks us to think about keeping watch until its historical close.

By expanding beyond the written word—without giving less attention to Scripture—the texts of the liturgy are powerful agents of social and moral change and become partners for the preacher. Again, the symbols we choose to live by can substantially alter our very worldview. The language to give God praise and thanksgiving "always and everywhere" stands in direct confrontation to the typical American "language of empire." The liturgy offers up a sacrifice through the One who offered himself up as a servant for all so that the many might be made whole. *It is not an exaggeration to say that if the culture of postmodernity fragments, it will be the Church's scriptural texts and liturgy that unify because it is in sacred Word and Worship that Christ gathers his people.* It should come as no surprise, then, that the Constitution on the Liturgy insists that the homily itself is part of the liturgy. By means of the Church's language and symbol, Christ offers himself in worship to the Eternal Father and exercises the work of redemption.

> In the liturgy the sanctification of man is manifested by signs perceptible to the senses, and is effected in a way which is proper to each of these signs; in the liturgy full public worship is performed by the Mystical Body of Jesus Christ, that is, by the head and His members.
>
> From this it follows that every liturgical celebration, because it is an action of Christ the priest and of His Body the Church, is a sacred action surpassing all others. No other action of the Church can match its claim to efficacy, nor equal the degree of it.[22]

Preaching in the context of the liturgy, then, recalls the whole work of our redemption and presents a unique opportunity to mediate meaning for the Christian assembly. For John Melloh, the preacher at the liturgy has the most natural of vocations, "offering to God what created beings can indeed offer, namely words of grateful loving acknowledgement." And so "to preach as a 'priest of the world' is to embrace the world—cosmos and all creation—and offer it to the Creator God in loving symbolic exchange. It implies rehearsing an attitude of thanksgiving in all of life, even its imperfection and yearning for completion; this is an 'eternal Eucharistic attitude.'"[23]

Clearly, the preacher needs to have an imagination to make use of these images and symbols, drawing on a rich treasure of human experiences inside and outside of ministry. *Failure to enable the congregation to envision together the gifts of God destined for the People of God often results in homilies that mirror the postmodern climate: they are themselves fragmented and without substance.* The corrective to incoherent homilies might appear to be moral instruction or heavily didactic preaching. But using moral dictums or pious instruction suggests that the preacher alone provides the meal for the Christian assembly. Furthermore, pious bromides do nothing to help cohere the congregation into unity and may fragment the hearers even further. We know from the liturgy itself that richer fare is for the community of the baptized to discover freely as children of God. As liturgist Martin Connell observes,

> Proclamation is rarely effective in revealing new insights about Jesus; rather, the efficacy of telling the familiar stories is realized through the local community's ordering and experience of proclaiming and hearing the narratives in the Liturgy of the Word, and in giving and receiving the body and blood of Christ. The Liturgy of the Word is not an educational opportunity, but a phenomenal, transformative, *saving* experience that unites reclusive, manic, depressed, erratic, possessed, infirm, lunatic, and dead people and makes of them a church.[24]

Indeed, allowing the faithful to unwrap the images and symbols in the liturgy and the scriptures from which they flow grants those gathered a full, active participation in the preaching event itself. Most important, the collective imagination of the Christian assembly forms a helpful counterbalance to the displacement of the "grand story" in postmodern culture. At the same time, this gathering of the congregation is hardly a stranger to theological foundation and doctrine. Doctrine, after all, emerges out of the theological imagination of the Church through its scriptures and its teachings to form a coherent historical link for the Christian community. Indeed, with a doctrinally informed, scripture-based preaching event, the homily leads the People of God precisely into the creedal formula: the baptized assembly's declaration "We believe in one God." This declaration is an affirmation of faith and an acknowledgment of the saving Lord's power of redemption in time. We have been gathered by what Mark Searle has called a "shared imagination," or "a common way of under-standing the world and our own place in it," so that we might believe more fully in what we have seen and heard. He continues:

> We need to recognize the importance of the imagina-tion as a source of belief, moral behavior, and even personal identity. Instead of didactic moralizing or even entertaining preaching, we need a rich diet of scriptural, traditional, and contemporary imagery, imagery which can help us discover our Christian iden-tity and become acutely aware of the difference between life lived before death and life lived after death, between the life of the good pagan and the rad-ical newness of the life lived in Christ.[25]

Finally, the imaginative gathering of the faithful into an "eternal Eucharistic attitude" takes place within a liturgical year, which is one of the greatest aids to preaching. The liturgical year offers the Christian community an alternative to secular time. To set our internal clocks by the Church year suggests that we are not controlled by the time that is passing away, but set our eyes instead on the lavish works of an eternal God who is beyond his-tory, even while accomplishing wonderful deeds within it.

> The patterns of worship and the sequence of readings continue inexorably, as ever, with the prayers and readings nearly the same as the last time they were proclaimed and heard a year ago, three years ago, a century or a millennium ago....The communal and sensory experience of people at worship always reveals God's love for creation and humanity, and how this love is mediated in the present experience of the rites and also in life apart from the church.[26]

PRACTICAL GUIDES FOR BIBLICAL AND LITURGICAL PREACHING

✔ Create a personal plan to read the whole Bible in three years or less.

When I took my first course on the Synoptic Gospels, I will never forget the experience of one our first assignments: to read the entire Gospel of Mark in one sitting. There was something about the pace, the character of Jesus, the sense of doubt of the disciples that made the reading of the whole Marcan account so vivid. Busy ministers these days are strapped for time and are lucky to get in a few minutes here and there for prayer or the Liturgy of the Hours. But as I suggested in the First Step on the Ladder of Preaching, nothing is more fundamental to the vocation of preaching than cultivating a personal relationship with the Lord and noticing in prayer how that unfolds in the midst of our pastoral care for the People of God. The wonderful and mysterious works of God become even more obvious if we devote our time to noticing those deeds in the narrative retelling in the Bible.

The parishioners we serve also have their collegial part to play in helping ministers understand the Word of God as it has been revealed to the whole Church. There are obvious advantages to parish-based scripture study groups that prayerfully consider the readings for the next Sunday. How do the faithful to whom I preach the Gospel witness a faith experience in their own lives? Undoubtedly, folks will bring their experience of the whole Bible with them; they will want to understand contexts for the various pericopes. Moreover, parishioners bring their own cultural contexts to the Sunday readings as well. What does the parable of the prodigal son mean to a mother who is struggling with a son with alcohol addiction? How does a wealthy CEO read the parable of Dives and Lazarus?

During these weekly study groups, it might be helpful to cultivate a fourfold process of *lectio divina* in which the minister and the people share the experience of reading the biblical text:

reading-listening, meditation, prayer, contemplation. We might take some time before the scripture study group meets, for instance, to engage this ancient process of *lectio divina*. Group members would then share their experiences when they meet to discuss the readings that week. In the first stage, we listen attentively to the words as they are written in the text. A good *reading out loud* (even in private!) of the Lectionary for the next Sunday will help launch this first phase. We take time, then, for the second phase, *meditation*. A deep hearing requires that we really "chew" on the words to see what they are doing; the process slows us down to engage the text deeply. Next, we take the moments that shine out for us to *prayer*, bringing to the Lord our own experience through the lens of these biblical moments. Finally, we remain still and wordless in *contemplation*, allowing God to love us just as we are—*where* we are. Such prayer experiences encourage us to see the biblical text as a bottomless well of prayer, in which life-giving connections might be made.

✔ Develop a pastoral plan for preaching the Sunday readings, the great feasts, and the saints.

If the liturgical year is so crucial, we ought not to let its presence go without using this great gift of the Church to enliven the hearts and minds of the people. Where do you want the parish to be at the end of the liturgical year? Or Advent? Or Lent? Or Easter? How will each season speak to the needs of the parish? Fr. James Wallace, a Redemptorist priest and professor of homiletics, suggests that preachers might attend to three "hungers" of the People of God in the liturgical homily. Taking his mandate from the conciliar documents and *Fulfilled in Your Hearing*, Wallace wrote the excellent book *Preaching to the Hungers of the Heart*, in which he invites the preacher to respond to the needs of the hearer in the context of the Church's liturgy. For Wallace, the central role of the homily for the new millennium remains facilitating the Word; that is, feeding God's People, but in specific ways, as suggested by the liturgical year:

First, the People of God *hunger for wholeness*. Drawing on the problems in a fragmented, postmodern culture without a central story, Wallace says that preaching the great feasts of the Lord satisfies one of the most basic human needs: "the hunger for a story that completes and makes us whole, offering a sense of being at peace in relation to oneself, others, the world and God."[27] That there is a story of salvation becomes clear in the mystery of preaching feasts like Christmas, where Jesus is the long-awaited Savior who came according to God's plan, in the fullness of time.

Second, we also *hunger for meaning*, and this need is satisfied by preaching within the sacramental rites, in which preaching is integral and crucial, "bridging the gap between *anamnesis* and *mimesis*, between remembering what God has done in the paschal mystery of Christ and what we are presently engaged in doing as an act of realizing the presence of salvation in our midst."[28]

Third, *our hunger extends to a yearning to belong*, and that is satisfied with the saints and Mary. Clearly, the saints and the mother of God have a unique mission to play in allowing the living Church to widen its community boundaries, "helping those at the Eucharistic assembly see themselves as part of a larger community of believers, past and present, all joining in the great act of praise and thanksgiving."[29] The inclusion of the saints in the liturgy and preaching about their lives as witnesses to God's saving work in the scriptures fosters a community of believers whose living baptismal faith is already present and deepening.

✔ *Find a personal metaphor for preaching at the liturgical rites.*

When we celebrate the sacraments with God's people, we are not just "dispensing" them, we are offering them life-giving, healing moments in the place of Christ for the purpose of building up the Church. Is there a way of understanding our ministerial function in human experience when it comes to these vital sacramental rites? When I celebrate funerals, for instance, I think of myself as a minister of hospitality, a graced innkeeper. Celebrating a funeral represents a potential opportunity for welcoming back an entire group of people at an extremely difficult time in their lives. As a celebrant during a funeral, it is the only time that I "answer the door," greet and console the people, and then lead them to the table of the Word and Sacrament. We offer words of comfort through the story of salvation and through the passion, death, and resurrection of Jesus. We feed our guests from the Eucharistic altar, a foretaste of the eternal banquet where all of God's children will dine one day. Lastly, we bless the guest of honor, who awaits the final rest. Our preaching offers words of comfort to these travelers who await the same place of rest in the Father's mansion. We send them on their way with hope and the comfort that the scripture and the liturgy provide.

MISSTEPS

✗ *Isolating passages or phrases out of context instead of speaking "through the Scriptures."*

As those charged to preach the Gospel, we may believe that our task centers around a kind of running commentary on the readings for the people who do not really know much about the Bible. It is not uncommon to hear preachers simply observing things about the readings one after the other: "In our first reading...and then the second reading...and so the Gospel...." The preacher is there to proclaim the Good News and not to offer an exegesis of the passages from the Lectionary. Still less is the one who preaches the Gospel to reduce the text to isolated phrases in order to champion some kind of moral agenda. Such tactics echo what *Fulfilled in Your Hearing* flags as those who believe that "the preacher's principle purpose is to interpret scriptural texts rather than communicate with real people, and that he interprets these texts primarily to extract ethical demands to impose on a congregation. Such preachers may offer good advice, but they are rarely heard as preachers of good news, and this very fact tends to distance them from their listeners."[30] Moreover, if the homily is an exercise in instruction or derivative examples, the Word of God becomes not a saving event, but a prescription or precept, rather like the sayings of Confucius.

These precepts are not necessarily terrible suggestions, of course, but how does such a practice enable the hearer to flourish and blossom after the Word has been sown? How does the homily serve to gather the assembly of faith? Ultimately, there is no reason to think that any listener would want to return to the whole story of salvation history after hearing a homily that has isolated a fragment of that narrative. *The basic question the homilist must answer here is how he engages all of scripture from the point of view of a faith experience in prayer.* If passages are simply isolated out of context, preaching on them is an invitation to a kind of knee-jerk application to everyday life, like *Chicken Soup for the Parochial Soul.*

✗ *Ignoring primary symbols either in Scripture or the liturgy.*

I remember a liturgy I attended once in a large parish where the altar was used as a kind of a catch-all for anything the presider decided to place on it—his glasses, a copy of the scriptures he carried around with him, the bulletin with the parish announcements, a black binder with the General Intercessions. Needless to say, that disregard for the primary symbol of Christ at the Eucharist skewed or confused the priorities of the worshipers. How does the preacher move from the ambo, where the Word is proclaimed, to the altar at which praise and thanksgiving are being offered when the latter now resembles more of an end table than a table of abundant blessing? When it comes to Scripture, the images and symbols ought to be mined and surfaced for their ongoing meaning as they pertain to the pastoral needs of the congregation. There is little use going on and on about the meaning of this or that image or symbol if it is just an exercise in "trivial pursuit." We don't really need to hear a long description about denarii and coinage in ancient Rome with no connection at all to the significance of why Jesus applied this particular image to the secular versus the sacred city. As we will see in later steps in the Ladder of Preaching, when exploring images in scripture, it is always absolutely necessary to return to the ears of the contemporary hearer: What might they make of this symbol and why does it matter to them right now?

QUESTIONS AND PROJECTS FOR CLASS

1. Ask students to share their experiences of narrative from a recent novel they have read or a movie they have seen. How does the narrative function as a single whole? What role does personal story play in their life?

2. Invite the international students to share their own experiences of narrative. What is their culture's story?

3. Ask one student to give a three-minute summary of salvation history to an imaginary youth group. Ask the class to discuss.

QUESTIONS FOR REFLECTION

1. Do I discuss the Bible as if it were a good story? What if I was retelling the story of David to a (fictional) group of people who had never heard of this Israelite hero before? How would I do it?

2. Write ten images that stand out in the Book of Genesis. What are they doing and how can you make them come alive?

3. What do you find consoling in the Church's liturgy? What do you find inspiring?

Step Three

CREATING A UNIFIED HOMILY

He wanders from one idea to another—no one central
point that you can take home.
　　—Mr. I. M. A. Disgruntled Catholic parishioner[1]

　　The question of homiletic unity follows closely on the heels
of Step One and Step Two in the Ladder of Preaching. Once the
foundational, relational steps have been undertaken, once the
preacher faces the question of his calling from God, once he truly
considers the people he serves and the scriptural and liturgical
texts that will gather them—there remains his task of fashioning
a unified homiletic text. The work of the Holy Spirit will be at
work in Christian preaching when we ask for God's help in sowing the Word in the field: scattering the seed amid all the various
kinds of soil that make up the human family. Yet Jesus' mandate
to preach the Good News to all nations requires that we develop,
not a "scattering" method of preaching, but a rhetorical method
to insure that listeners maximize the Word and yield abundant
fruit. As St. Augustine reminds us:

> The interpreter and teacher of the divine scriptures,
> therefore, the defender of right faith and the hammer
> of error, has the duty of both teaching what is good
> and unteaching what is bad; and in this task of speak-
> ing it is his duty to win over the hostile, to stir up the

slack, to point out to the ignorant what is at stake and
what they ought to be looking for.[2]

So then it is up to the preacher to develop a language or method
that will gather the People of God into the one living sacrifice of
praise during the liturgical homily—no matter what their dispo-
sition. This is a tall order! How do we meet the congregation
where they are, while weaving a homiletic tapestry that is rich
biblically and theologically?

PREACHING IN THEIR MIDST

Good preaching reaches people where they are, not where
we wish they would be. That is not to say that preachers do not
challenge or inspire, but that *they lead the Christian assembly
through a process of arrival through the gift of the Spirit: from
wherever they find themselves to praise and thanksgiving, compassion and understanding.* In the past, it was not uncommon for
sermons to state a series of (three) points and then have some
kind of conclusion. Most often, these were topical, deductive sermons that concentrated on distilling certain aspects of the faith
or life that may or may not have been drawn from the scriptures.
Or these points may have been taken from the scriptures and
applied as an analogy for improving Christian living.

For example, a homily on the prodigal son parable might be
structured around this: (1) The younger son rebelled; (2) he
regretted; (3) he returned. These three Rs are part of our own
lives. There are times when we rebel. We want our own way…But
then we see what happens to this useless resistance from God's
ways…And we return."

The analogy here is simply deduction: the prodigal son does
this, and so do I; therefore, I am just like the younger son.
Nobody is going to disclaim the observations about this famous
parable and these points about the younger son. There is not
much to argue here, but there is also not much room to grow
either. The homily with the three Rs exists on the level of cogni-

tion; no one is really challenged to do what the parable itself is extending: an invitation to conversion.

On the other hand, if the homily were to acknowledge the listener, that dynamic would tend to suggest that the text carries a certain amount of elasticity about it. The biblical world needs to be stretched out and its meaning pondered in the context of the historical reality of the Christian community. It is, after all, this *specific* group of people, these congregants that wait upon the Word; *the congregation has specific needs and will unlock the biblical text from their own horizon.* Many preachers, though, are tempted to perform the homily with little attention to the listener, as if the group of people in front of them were supposed to eavesdrop on a private meditation. "How easy it is for us to preach out of our own experience, imagining that it is everyone's instead of the socially-located, historically-situated, cast-bound one that it really is. When we universalize our experience as if it were the key signature of all our hearers, we deny both the limitations of our voice and the repertoire of our hearers."[3] Simply stating an observation about the text and creating an analogy does not provide for the pastoral contingencies of *this* time and *this* place with *these* people. As *Fulfilled in Your Hearing* says,

> Another way of structuring the homily, and one that is more in keeping with its function of enabling people to celebrate the liturgy with deepened faith, is to begin with a description of a contemporary human situation which is evoked by the scriptural texts, rather than with an interpretation or reiteration of the text. After the human situation has been addressed, the homilist can turn to the Scriptures to interpret this situation, showing how the God described therein is also present and active in our lives today. The conclusion of the homily can then be an invitation to praise this God who wills to be lovingly and powerfully present in the lives of his people.[4]

Now *Fulfilled in Your Hearing* suggests only one of the many ways in which a preacher may approach the homily (beginning with a contemporary situation), but the document also recommends that *the structure of the homily be organized around the hearer*. This particular point cannot be stressed enough because grasping its fundamental meaning is at the heart of good contemporary preaching. To connect with a hearer from the beginning suggests an *inductive method* that moves along a general pattern from specific experience to a general conclusion. In contrast to the often abstract rhetorical tactics of a deductive homily,

> the inductive sermon creates tension: the congregation recognizes unresolved qualities in understanding a biblical text, doctrine, practice, or situation and seeks to know how those tensions can be resolved. Inductive preaching is itself an experience of discovery. In this respect, inductive movement reflects the movement of many human experiences.[5]

The inductive homily is a process by definition; it encourages the Christian assembly to participate in the unfolding of the Word in their midst, thereby deepening a faith that is already present through baptism. Induction trusts the assembly to hear the Word of God. They participate not by an analogy created by the preacher, but in a response in freedom and creativity.

It is the task of the homilist, then, to discover an inductive method that is not only going to gather the assembly, but will keep the assembly engaged in the Word of God. Ultimately, effective homiletics will be the language that shapes the Christian assembly into unity.

By unity I do not mean that everyone is thinking the same thing, or having an identical faith experience; the congregation will individually respond freely in their own way with questions, challenges, and affirmations. By unity I mean simply that the homiletic text has gathered the People of God around the Word,

Christ himself. On a more practical level, if the people fail to hear the message of the homily, it may very well be, not that they have failed to listen, but that the preaching event has not reached their ears. Being aware of the listener and what these hearers of the Gospel make of my homily is the point of departure for contemporary homiletics. As master homiletician Fred Craddock explains:

> It is vital to our task that we be aware that the experience of listening is not a secondary consideration after we have done our exegesis of the texts and theological exploration. The listener is present from the beginning. The Christian tradition, biblical and extra-biblical, came to us from those who heard it, and we hear it and pass it on to other hearers. The stamp of listening and the listenability of the message is on it when we get it, and in telling it, we confirm that it is listenable.[6]

The task of sowing is up to the preacher and it is for God to grant the increase. As Paul tells the Corinthians, "I planted, Apollos watered, but God gave the growth. So neither the one who plants nor the one who waters is anything, but only God who gives the growth. The one who plants and the one who waters have a common purpose, and each will receive wages according to the labor of each. For we are God's servants, working together; you are God's field, God's building" (1 Cor 3:6–9). Listening with the ears of the heart is the graced experience of proclamation.

PREACHING WITH THE HEARER IN MIND

We have already noted the inseparable connection between preaching and pastoring. Preaching's pastoral mandate begs this question: How can we consider a plan for writing a homily that preaches through the scriptures with a focus on the listener? We may know very well what the passage in the scriptures has to tell us, but what is going to be the method that best allows the Christian assembly to unpack the living Word of God unfolding in their midst? Most elementary, we need to make sure that the idea on which we intend to preach reaches the ears of the faithful. In many cases, the preacher has a lot of insights into the text, but lacks a formal apparatus that will enable the listeners to grasp the entirety of what is being said. The necessity of the sermon form should be obvious if the preacher wants a unified text. The preacher may be sincere in following Steps One and Two in the Ladder of Preaching, but needs to recognize that rhetoric has a vital part to play in the craft of a homily. As John of the Cross tells us, "Elegant style and delivery lift up and restore even those things that have fallen into ruin, just as poor presentation spoils what is good and destroys."[7] In light of the importance of the formal aspects of the homily, what might be a unifying experience of gathering around the Word of God; what might be an inductive method that might shape the crucial interplay between text, congregation, and preacher?

Thomas Long has created a formal system for the sermon that has been helpful to many preachers and that establishes a solid alliance between the world of the biblical text and those who hear the Word. In his book *The Witness of Preaching*, Long develops a simple method that he calls *form and function* that helps to unify the homiletic process. As a Presbyterian minister, Long intends his sermon form to be for longer sermons, but this strategy could be adapted to the Catholic Sunday homily as well. Long says:

> The place to begin in creating a sermon form is with the focus and the function—what the sermon aims to say and to do. If we keep our eye firmly on these, the sermon form will have unity, since the whole sermon will be shaped to accomplish these aims. [In] everything the sermon needs to accomplish the focus and function should be included in the structure, and any-

thing that does not help us to achieve these aims is extraneous and should be weeded out.[8]

As an example, Long suggests that we take a look at Romans 8:28–39. Now there are many things that might strike us when reading this powerful Pauline text: its beauty, its sheer theological weight and depth, its ability to speak to us even today. There are so many quotable lines that we might be tempted to pull out just one or two and center our attention on these. But that is not what Long has in mind. The focus of the homily must begin to establish the *claim* of the text. What is this particular text saying to us? *The preacher must settle on a single claim* and not be tempted to get too complicated or go on to different topics—all of which may be very inviting for so rich a biblical passage. For Long, the claim in Romans 8:28–39 is this: "Because we have seen in Jesus Christ that God is for us, we can be confident that God loves and cares for us even when our experience seems to deny it."[9] Notice that the focus statement is relatively short, not a series of compound sentences or endless dependent clauses. The claim of the text should be a simple and direct one.

At the same time, the passage is not only *saying* something, it wants to *do* something. As a text it has a particular claim, but those words are also reaching out to take hold of a listener as well. God's Word is living and active. And so there is an invitation to create a second part to the sermon form, which emerges naturally from its focus. The function will be the very operation that engages the active and creative powers of the listeners. In writing the focus statement, the preacher concentrates on the claim of the text. Now, when creating its function statement, he uncovers the text's power over the hearer. With Long's previous focus statement in mind, he says that the function that follows is "to reassure and give hope to troubled hearers in the midst of their distress."[10]

The function statements will always be closely connected to the focus statements and will usually contain active verbs that engage the congregation: to *provoke* the hearers; to *instill* in the listener; to *give* hope, and so on. *These functions are the tactics or the process by which the preacher will move his congregation to the intended goal*—reassurance and hope in distress—based on the biblical claim in Romans 8:28–39. If the homily is successful,

> the preacher will have enabled the hearers to move from wherever they were at the start of the sermon to a new place, a place of reassurance and hope in the midst of their distress, because they have heard the sermon's focus: "God is for us; we can be confident that God loves and cares for us even when our experience seems to deny it."[11]

A true test case of a good homily is whether or not the assembly can state in a single sentence the focus statement as intended by the preacher at the end of the homily. In a word, the focus answers the question, "What did you hear?" The next time someone in the congregation says, "Father Bill, that was a great homily!" or, "Deacon Smith, I enjoyed your preaching," the daring homilist should ask in response: "What did you hear?"

In my introduction classes on preaching and in workshops, I have found that using a focus and function are useful points of departure for emerging preachers. Why? Because these formal guides of focus and function are not only valuable ways of creating an alliance between the meaning of the biblical text and what that scripture wants to claim on the Christian hearer, but they also maintain values that will be vitally important to observe during a lifetime of preaching: a strong reading of Scripture and Tradition, attention to the hearer, homiletic unity.

It should be obvious that the preaching event ought to occur through the scriptures and mediated through the interpretation of the preacher. If they are constructed with the focus statement in mind, the function forms a guarantee that the Christian assembly will be the beneficiaries of the blessings of the

Word of God. Additionally, this scriptural reading clearly allows the assembly to participate in the Word of God with the preacher. The full and active participation that the liturgy encourages does not suddenly take a back seat during the homily when the congregation is supposed to become passive. No, the baptized assembly wants to engage in a faith moment in which, in Long's terms, they are reassured and given hope in troubled times. In the end, this comfort does not come from the preacher, of course, but from the Word of God itself.

Long clearly has the hearer in mind when deploying his sermon form. The focus and the function statements form an active claim on the hearer. These are not observations on the text or commentaries on the Bible, but living intentions or destinies meant to transform the listener. The biblical text has a trajectory because it is organic and living, and its goal is the ears and hearts of the People of God. That experience of the Word is facilitated by the interpreter-preacher, who sows the seed in a ground that he has enriched by careful attention to the inductive form of the homily. As Fred Craddock says, "The task of the interpreter is not to transform, explain, apply, or otherwise build bridges from the text to the listeners. Rather, the task is to release the text upon the listener's ear by translating it into the language of the listener."[12] Using the imagination of the listener and the invention of the preacher, it is the Holy Spirit that transforms the People of God by the Word made Flesh, the living image of the Father's glory.

THE UNITY OF THE HOMILY

The importance of scriptural and hearer-centered preaching notwithstanding, there is probably nothing more crucial to engaging a congregation of hearers than homiletic unity. According to the late Bishop Ken Untener, "too many thoughts" remains "the most frequently voiced complain about homilies, a runaway for first place."[13] It is easy to see how many homilies get hung up on this issue of too many thoughts. As a result, homilies often struggle to say what they want to say as a summary in a single declarative sentence, complicated by the writing and thinking process. It is no secret that we live in the information age and some homilies tend to mirror this cultural reality, reading like a grocery list of observations that move from topic to topic, a kind of list produced by a Google search. The tendency to use disconnected thoughts is particularly true if the homily is not anchored to a text, but preached more or less spontaneously. Chances are that the multiplication of thoughts makes sense to the preacher himself, but not to the "group mind" of the congregation, whose ability to track such scatterings are slower compared to individual reception.

I have already mentioned the well-known strategy of teaching homiletics by deploying the use of three points and a conclusion. As Untener suggests, using three points might be fine in establishing a *kind* of unity, if they are somehow (artificially) connected to each other. The previous example of a homily on the prodigal son maintains some kind of unity simply because of common characteristics: rebellion, regretfulness, and repentance all begin with R and all are qualities of the younger son we are observing. But three points often show up as just that: three points. They are just informative facts or things to be dispensed, nuggets that are fashioned as characteristic of this or that passage. I would say that using three informational pieces, cleverly arranged, will create a *false sense of unity in language only*, but not necessarily a coherent text gathered around the hearer of the Word, who listens with the "ears of the heart." It is unlikely that such a schema would ignite a unified process of engagement on the part of the congregation.

Thinking of the biblical parable of the merchant who sells all he has for a pearl of great price, Untener recommends the metaphor of a pearl because "it is something worth listening to....It simply conveys a profound truth in a way that we all realize it with a clarity we didn't have before. *Pearl* also expresses compactness, compression, unity."[14] Significantly, Untener distinguishes his "one pearl" from "one theme." "If a homily is united simply by a common theme, it usually moves horizontally at a surface level from one thought to another and [it] results in too many thoughts and little depth; if a homily revolves around a pearl, it goes vertically into the depth of one thought."[15] Again, the theme might exist on the level of language, but not take the baptized assembly through a process. In summary, the pearl invites exploration through imagery and depth of purpose; it is meant for the homily typified by *Fulfilled in Your Hearing* which asks that the homily deepen the faith of the congregation and enliven the commitment of the baptized assembly, while the theme stays relatively static and unsatisfying on the level of faith.

To make his point, Untener contrasts two examples of sketches of homilies on the following Gospel text: "You are the light of the world....Your light must shine before others that they may see your good deeds and glorify your heavenly Father" (Matt 5:14, 16; NAB).

Preaching on a theme:

I'm going to talk about how we are called to give witness to our faith. We need to stand up for our faith whether we're at home, at work, at school, with our friends. Peter and Paul were willing to do that—they both died as martyrs—and people down through the centuries have done the same. There are martyrs today too. Too often we take our faith for granted and don't realize that we are often out of step with the world around us. We need to give witness to that.[16]

Untener suggests that this example shows no focus and is a tissue of clichés. Actually, from the point of view of Thomas Long, the example also lacks *function*. What is the *action word* that we could use to describe the *intention* of the passage on the hearer? If the focus is about witnessing to the Gospel, how are we as an assembly led into this testimony? From my perspective, the real tip-off that there is no function statement—or, for that matter, that the congregation has not been invited to claim their own power of witness for themselves—is the predominance of imperatives: "We *need to* stand up for our faith" or, "We *need to* give witness"—both of which are likely heard as "*you must...*" *The point of the function is to want to give witness.* That desire is what the action verbs like "encourage" the congregation or "inspire" the assembly are all about. Ultimately, the Christian assembly will be brought to want and desire, otherwise the preacher becomes an old schoolmaster shaking his finger at the children and telling them what they need to do in order to be good.

Untener's other example, using the same Gospel text, uses a different tactic altogether.

Preaching on one pearl:

I'm going to use the image of daytime running lights on cars. Their purpose is so others can see the car rather than vice versa. People have "running lights" too, from the moment they get out of bed in the morning. Others see our "running lights" whether we intend it or not. We need to take a good look at what they see.[17]

Although this example also uses "We need," it is an invitation into further reflection, to ponder a problem posed in the image. We need to probe deeply into ourselves and look at the quality of our "running lights." There is no imperious tone or sense that we have an abstract standard that we need to live up to—"We need to give witness to that." The use of probing our "running lights" could well have a function behind it: "to inspire the people to reflect on their ability to shine before others" or, "to engage the congregation in a conscious awareness of how their lights shine before the world." The one pearl, then, seems to suggest the focus and function recommended by Long. The trajectory of the homily is a process of deepening a faith commitment mediated by the preacher, allowing the congregation to self-reflect not in abstract terms but concretely and personally.

I will also observe that the strategy behind unity in the homily is not only rhetorical; it is also theological. If the homily is intended to lead the Christian assembly into more thoughtful and reflective worship, then gathering them by words is essential. In a certain sense, we express in the homily the unity of gesture intended by the liturgy itself, and the arena of language becomes the forum of communion and fellowship. The experience will be echoed during the "second epiclesis" when the presider in Eucharistic Prayer III asks the Father, "Grant that we, who are nourished by his body and blood, may be filled with his Holy Spirit, and become one body, one spirit in Christ." A homily that is scattered suggests a flock that is confused, disordered, and wayward; that is hardly the focal point of Christian gathering as a Eucharistic, liturgical assembly. Additionally, as I hinted earlier, we know that following the Sunday homily the Christian assembly professes their faith in one God as one holy Catholic Church. Therefore, the homily allows the faithful to witness that very gathering of unity through the theological clarity of the homily. As Stephen DeLeers points out:

> As we preach God's Word, we clarify for our people who God is, how God has worked in Jesus to save us, and how God's Spirit continues this work in our midst today. We clarify our identity as Church and all that entails. We reflect on the wonderful gifts of Word and Sacrament, Christ-bearers for God's people. Our central homiletic point continually revisits these core beliefs of Christians as they emerge from the Scriptures. The further down the hierarchy of truths we descend, the less likely that our point will be worth making.[18]

The Creed, which immediately follows the homily, is a clear expression of our unity as a Church. For DeLeers, clarity—the development of one central point—is one of the pillars in his description of what makes a good homily.[19] Such clarity becomes vital for the listener if the homily is to be pastorally and theologically effective.

IN THE BEGINNING: PROBLEMS WITH HOMILETIC UNITY

The problem of unity in the homily often begins from the very start. Introductions are absolutely crucial in setting the tone, the pace, and the overall direction of the homily. As such, the introduction itself needs to be composed with a sense of organic unity and with the recognition that it is at the service of the rest of the homily. Here is an introduction* that starts out fine, but then becomes misdirected.

> Flannery O'Connor's short stories are populated by a world of grotesques who often reveal some hidden truths. In O'Connor's story "The River," a young boy attends an evangelical revival meeting and decides to be baptized. "You won't be the same again," the preacher tells him. "You'll count." Harry, now christened "Bevel," wants to lay his pain "in the River of Faith, in the River of Life, in the River of Love, in the rich and red river of Jesus' Blood...in the movement toward the Kingdom of Christ." As it happens, Bevel takes the search for the Kingdom of Christ and the life of grace very seriously. *That is important for all of us to do because discovery of the Holy in our midst is important for all the Baptized.*

*All partial or full homilies that appear in boxes have been written by the author.

And so the boy goes back to the river, not to fool with preachers any more, but to baptize himself, and to keep on going until he finds the Kingdom of Christ. As the story closes, the last sentences leave us stunned, even depressed as to the boy's fate. "He plunged under once and this time, the waiting current caught him like a long gentle hand and pulled him swiftly forward and down. For an instant he was overcome with surprise; then since he was moving quickly and knew that he was getting somewhere, all his fury and his fear left him."[20]

It is amazing what just one sentence will do to derail a more or less unified process. The preacher would do well to eliminate the middle (italicized) sentence of the paragraph; it needlessly diverts our attention away from the rest of the story and introduces a rhetorical element quite different from the overall pattern of the rest of the paragraph. If we are following a particular trajectory, we expect to be introduced to something at the end of such a prelude. If the introductory paragraph wanders around, the congregation will not be at all clear about where they are supposed to be headed. Subject scattering is never helpful to introductions, especially when sentences are introduced that split the congregation into various detours along the way, inviting them to think about this and that. Introductions need a sharp focus or they are counterproductive.

The other initial difficulty with unity concerns the transition from the introduction to the first section of the homily. Ideally, there should be a seamless, absolute, and necessary connection between the introduction and the initial foray into the body of the homily. Consider this connection, for instance, taken from the same homily for the Feast of the Lord's Baptism and following the introduction given above.

[End of introduction]..."Then since he was moving quickly and knew that he was getting somewhere, all his fury and his fear left him."

[Beginning of section one of homily] The waters of baptism are supposed to kill us. It is not by accident that the Church has never permitted just a sprinkling for those to be baptized. Indeed, if we would view one of the exquisite examples of baptisteries from antiquity, like San Giovanni in Pisa, for instance, we'd see just how high those waters reach.

We might note here that the introduction and the passage that follows are tightly linked. That linkage between the introduction and the first stage of the homily provides the reason for the introduction in the first place. If the movement between these two areas becomes short-circuited, the congregation will scatter. Moreover, the initial sentence in the first stage of the homily has been dramatically anticipated by the introduction and sets the motion going for the rest of the text; it cues the congregation that this homily will be moving in this particular direction. So here again, the coherence of the introduction becomes crucial. Therefore, *where the homily is going is always intentional and never just a series of casual observations.*

While on this topic, I want to highlight the *tension* in in*tention*ality: the preacher knows exactly where he is going, but deliberately keeps a certain tension going in the homily from the very first lines. We can just imagine the impact on a listener who hears, "The waters of baptism are supposed to kill us." Questions are immediately posed underneath this line: "What did he mean by that—baptism is the source of life, isn't it?" "How could that be? Tell me more." These are participative, indeed, collaborative, inquiries on the part of the Christian assembly, a kind of "silent dialogue," if you will, in the homiletic act; they are guiding questions that face every good homily that is structured around narrative unity or, more specifically, plot. These questions are crucial, silent witnesses to the inductive process. With a well-plotted homily, the preacher can be sure of an organic structure that engages the Christian assembly in a crucial dialogue of discovery where the Word is gradually unwrapped like a rare gift. The Christian assembly then finds itself freely receiving the grace of the Word in their midst. Plot guarantees that there will be coherence in the homiletic text.

THE PLOT AND THE PREACHER

In the best-case scenarios, the preacher involves the congregation in a narrative process guided by a well-plotted homily. The question of clarity and unity in my mind concerns an inner dynamism that gathers around the mechanics and strategies of the classic Western plot.[21] Mary Catherine Hilkert reminds us that preachers function very much like narrators. "The preacher's configuring of the plot of the homily is an act of creative imagination that tends toward a future beyond human conception."[22]

A strategically plotted homily that signals its movement from the start is *economic and ergonomic*: it intentionally moves as a linear trajectory to a climax and then a closure. Homilies that are well plotted have an inner coherence with a beginning, middle, and end. When we stop to think about it, tension and relaxation are basic to the core of our biological life, fundamental to who we are as human beings. Harmonic tonal systems in music are based on hierarchical pitches that involve tension and relaxation; they move toward resolution. The Church's liturgy is a drama of tensions and relaxations as well. Building a homily that is well plotted is essential to the listener's experience and is a mirror of the way we understand salvation history: "What we have heard from the beginning is this." Or again, "In the fullness of time, God sent his only Son."

The climax of the homiletic plot is shaped around the Word, who has entered into human history, where it continues to be released in its fullness. Homilies become crafted as narrational moments that lead the People of God into a deeper discovery of the Word made visible. To preach with a sense of plot guiding the homily allows the congregation to sense that they are in a world of coherence at the Eucharistic Liturgy, that God has gathered his people together. What better gift could we ask for in a postmodern environment that tends toward dismantling and fragmentation than a homily that knows where it's going? In a well-plotted homily, God's Word becomes the point of illumination for those who are looking for the light.

If we consider the classical Aristotelian plot structure, then we are dealing with the *arrangement of material*—an order that follows a particular causation. If the homily does not cohere around a focus statement or, more particularly, a "pearl" as Untener suggests, then the result will be scattered. A nice story here and there, or a wise exegetical point made about the readings, does not serve to gather the people in a narrative process. It might be useful to think of the formal aspects of the plotted homily as something like a Hollywood movie. Films are always designed with the spectator in mind. Think of the last movie you saw either in the theater or on a rented DVD. Did the first ten minutes flounder? Probably not. Even in bad movies, the filmmakers realize that it is important to get the plot mechanism going immediately. In the famous detective movies of the 1940s, such as John Huston's *The Maltese Falcon* (1941) or Otto Preminger's *Laura* (1944), a detective encounters a series of questions that become our own: "Who killed Miles Archer?" "Who killed Laura Hunt?" Those questions drive us toward the end of the film.

Plotted homilies involve the congregation in dramatic tension, which keeps them engaged in the preaching. As I have already suggested, it is naïve to think that groups of people will come to the Eucharist every Sunday with the burdens and concerns that weigh them down and listen to a rambling preacher's thoughts. Good homiletics requires rhetorical skills that face the needs of the contemporary culture squarely in the face. The sober fact is that what *does* hold people captive each week is the entertainment industry. That certainly does not mean that the homily or the liturgy should be entertaining or telling people what they want to hear. It does mean finding a way through an appropriate rhetorical form to keep the Christian assembly suitably engaged in order that the Word might unfold before them and that they will hear what they *need* to hear. Tension in plot waits for the homily to find a resolution, much like a good mystery novel or film. In a certain sense, from the very beginning the preacher is posing a problem that he and the congregation will solve together:

> Palm Sunday is a lot like the snow on our lilacs. We celebrate today not some neat lesson nor a clear-cut article of faith but a paradox, a mystery, a mingling of forces both good and evil, both glorious and cruel. We begin with a brassy march into Jerusalem. With palms in our hands and praise on our lips:
> "Blessed is he who comes in the name of the Lord!" But in a few minutes there will be a chill in the air when we will cry out, "Crucify him! Crucify him!"[23]

When Robert Waznak preached this homily on Palm Sunday, he took the advice given in the *Sacramentary* that a brief homily may be preached after the reading of the Lord's Passion. This portion of Waznak's text immediately follows the introduction and it is notable for its compact, subtle, dramatic tension and movement. It recalls the hosannas raised at the beginning of the week and ends with the murderous shouts of Good Friday; it recapitulates the powerful emotions that course through the week, inviting the congregation to see itself in motion as the week unfolds. As it invokes the chronology of the week, the homiletic text becomes an invitation to mystery, a call to participate in Holy Week. And the image that sets the stage from the beginning is "snow on lilacs." That picture is a plot set in motion that begs the question: "Would you unlock this image for us?" And again, "How is snow on lilacs like Palm Sunday?" The dramatic tension is evoked by the preacher who begins to spin a narrative in order to captivate the hearers.

Another advantage to plot is that it moves the narrative toward closure. Since causation is at the root of how plots work, its structure implicates us in waiting for an ending. In E. M. Forster's classic literary work *Aspects of the Novel,* he reminded his readers that there is a difference between a story, a kind of snapshot of life, and a plot. He said that "the king died and then the queen died" is a story. But "the king died and then the queen died of grief" is a plot. There is an underlying question of causation in the second example: the question "why?" "Grief" provides the cause and we want to know more.[24] *The implication of plot is already imbedded in well-defined focus and function statements: the focus expresses the intention of the homily and the function bears its strategy and supplies its causation.* The plot of the homily arranges how the focus/function will be carried out in process. A good guiding principle when constructing homilies around plot is to think of the congregation with a question on their lips: "What is next?" That is the question of anticipation. If they have a sense of salvation history, then the Christian assembly is already waiting for the Word to be fulfilled in their hearing, for the eschatological consummation of God's promise. We are a creation that groans with eager longing. Obviously, in creating a sense of closure through dramatic tension, we are engaging in a narrative process that takes us beyond merely observing certain points about the readings on a given day. The bottom line for preachers is to remember that narrative is fundamental to the human experience and to the way in which God has revealed himself to the world.

PRACTICAL EXERCISES FOR CREATING HOMILETIC UNITY

Tom Long designed his focus and function strategy for Sunday sermons, but there is no reason why this operation could not be applied to shorter homilies, particularly on weekdays.

✔ *Try consistently using a focus and function strategy with daily homilies.*

Here is a daily homily on Luke 13:10–17 (Monday in the Thirteenth Week in Ordinary Time) with a very clear focus statement as the first sentence.

[Focus:] Kindness never takes a holiday, not even the Sabbath. Jesus' cure reminds the Pharisees and us that the law of charity prevails over everything. Acts of love erase any kind of human law, even the ones that justify us.

[Function: to encourage the listeners to respond to the demands of charity and help them think of simple ways that lead to God.] There is a true story about a middle-aged Jewish woman—I'll call her Eva—who survived the unimaginable horror of the concentration camps at Auschwitz. When the American army came to liberate the prisoners, Eva was still able to get around a bit. So one of the captains asked her to show him around, and so she did. Years later, Eva was asked to remember her time at Auschwitz, especially the last days, the moments of liberation and freedom. Although still lively and intelligent, she said very little about the camp and, indeed, those final hours. She did, however, remember one thing very clearly. Recalling the young captain who asked Eva to show him around, she said, "He held the door for me." That was a gesture meant for one human toward another she had almost forgotten.

> The lessons of love transcend a thousand midnights and as many nightmares. Jesus' first instinct with the man who is sick is to cure him no matter what the condition. Jesus transforms people's lives by the hand of divine charity. In so doing, Christ has called us out of darkness into light. And at the hour of our death, we might find ourselves easily slipping through the gates of paradise, only because "he held the door for me."

The focus is fairly obvious because it is the first statement, something like a "topic sentence." Also, the function is articulated almost immediately after we learn the focus, engaging us in the outcome that has been projected. This homily is less than three minutes long and has a single pearl, which the focus statement itself encapsulates. Research conducted by Untener and others supports the fact that listeners favor the weekday homily because it usually sticks with one idea. We can find useful examples in daily preaching that will help guide us into the Sunday homily.

✔ Murder your darlings.

This is very common advice to writers: cut what you don't need. If there is anything that is going to sink a potentially good homily it is words—too many of them and in the wrong places. Remember what Eliza Doolittle sings in *My Fair Lady*? "I get words all day through, first from him, now from you. Is that all you blighters can do?" When explaining the term *murder your darlings* to my homiletic students, I usually point to Euripides' classical Greek tragedy *Medea*. Drawing from Greek mythology, Euripides showcased Medea as a woman who was wronged by her husband, Jason, who left her for a princess. For revenge, Medea made the princess a golden dress and a crown that caused the unfortunate woman to burst into flames. In order to exact a more pitiless revenge, Medea also killed her two sons, Mermeros and Pheres. Thus, she murdered her darlings for a more deadly, horrific revenge on her adulterous husband. She certainly made her point well by doing away with what she loved most.

Similarly, homilists may have lovely "children" that they have brought to light and want desperately to share with the congregation. Put these jewels away and hide them in a box on an index card for another homily. Rarely can a homily be too economical. Are these precisely the most-correct, well-placed words to get the message across? We simply don't need five illustrations when one will due. There is something wrong when the introduction takes up almost half the homily or we feel the need to tell one more story or give yet another illustration. We need to ask a fundamental question related to economy of writing: Does this language move the homily along toward an ending? Does less verbiage do a better job? If it is not really necessary, cut it out or else we will find ourselves with what American novelist Henry James referred to, in another context, as "a loose baggy monster."

✔ Be conscious of how plots work in media.

I will have more to say about this in another step on the Ladder of Preaching, but it is always worth attending to the dynamics of plot in popular culture in order to attend to the pastoral needs of the listeners. What is the rhetorical strategy of television commercials? What is the plot? How does a Hollywood feature film move us along? How are we hooked?

Preachers cannot afford to be passive spectators of popular culture. The people we serve are consuming mass culture all week. What is the frame of reference that they are absorbing and how does it shape them? Above all, get a sense of drama: Go to a play. Read a novel. What makes good dramatic structure work, and how does that translate into a homily?

MISSTEPS

✗ *Not acknowledging the homily as a unifying and inductive process of engagement for the hearers.*

If we think that the homily is a series of points or reflections, then we are missing the opportunity to deepen the faith experience of the Christian assembly through a process of listening. If we preach deductively, do we really want the congregation to come away with a series of points that they could just as well extract over the Internet? Why come to worship just to get information? Other difficulties follow from this initial misstep which we have already discussed in some detail. Moreover, since deductive homilies, or preaching that is organized by what Untener calls "theme," never presume to have the hearer in mind, there is no guarantee that the homily will engage anyone at all. Deduction invites scattered details that deal with a thin layer of meaning and could wander into abstractions. The degree to which the homily fails to engage is usually the degree to which there is extraneous material, disordered and poorly arranged for the listener. The common fault of this misstep is often the neglect of the previous two steps, which are conscious of the hearer's role in the preaching act. After all, if the homily is not structured around the listener, chances are that the unity that is so crucial to its reception will not occur.

✗ *String of pearls.*

This problem is a combination of several things: having too much to say, not knowing how to cut or edit our seemingly important ideas, not understanding the focus and the function. The result: a string of what could be well-developed pearls but that turn out instead to be a loose string of ideas, pearls that are not "cultured" or developed. I once heard homilies like this described as "Greeting Card Homiletics." They are disconnected thoughts waiting to be shaped into some kind of narrative form.

QUESTIONS AND PROJECTS FOR CLASS

1. After a student preaches a homily, ask the class to name the focus statement. Is this what the preacher had in mind?

2. After the same homily, ask the students to name what they feel the homily motivated them to do. Then ask the preacher to name the function statement.

3. Ask the preacher what he would change in order to discover the "pearl" in his homily.

4. Record the student's homily on video tape and ask him to revise it with an eye toward "murdering his darlings."

QUESTIONS FOR REFLECTION

1. How do I go about discovering the central idea or claim of a biblical text? Once I do that, what is my method for bringing that idea to the congregation?

2. How many things did I say in my last homily? Revise it with one focus. What is the result?

3. How do I experience myself as a narrator when I preach? Do I gather the assembly together during my homily?

Step Four

FINDING A HOMILETIC METHOD

My sermon on the meaning of the manna in the
Wilderness can be adapted to almost any occasion,
joyful, or, as in the present case, distressing.
—Oscar Wilde, *The Importance of Being Earnest*
(1895)

St. Francis de Sales was a great proponent of homiletic
method, a feature much lacking in contemporary Catholic preaching. "We must adhere to method in all things," Francis wrote.
"There is nothing that is more helpful to a preacher, makes his
preaching more profitable, and is so pleasing to his hearers."[1]
The unity of the homily will always be better served when we
find an appropriate method that structures our preaching.
Homiletic methods exist for both the preacher and the congregation. A good method helps the preacher to draw disparate
thoughts into a unified whole. Methodology allows the process
of preaching to be a discovery of the Word made visible. We
might very well have powerful insights and prayer experiences
around the *Sunday Lectionary* readings, but wonder how to
organize these observations and experiences in a systematic way
around the listener.

Deploying an effective method for our homilies permits the preacher to create texts for hearers. Homiletic method allows preachers to substantially own biblical texts for preaching and unpack them for the Christian assembly. Those who have developed appropriate organizational tools for preaching recognize that these armatures are structured for the ears of the faithful. Some professors of preaching believe that homiletic form has suffered years of neglect for the sake of content. And yet, paradoxically, the content goes unheard because it is poorly organized, lacks a narrative dynamic, and does not adhere to the listener. As Paul Scott Wilson tells us, "Preachers have tended to think that sermon form is secondary to sermon content or even that form is largely irrelevant; yet, ineffective sermon form pervades and distorts the theological content like a computer virus that infects every file....As a result, the gospel of Jesus Christ suffers."[2] Contemporary homiletic methods are rhetorical skills, lively systems that can be adapted and used in preaching during many different contexts and circumstances. *Fulfilled in Your Hearing* says it quite clearly: "Every art is based on a theory and a method, and preaching is no exception."[3] As I have already suggested in the previous step, the focus and function statements are a kind of method or strategy. But there are others that require our more extended attention. This step will take us into an examination of three such homiletic methods.

DAVID BUTTRICK'S HOMILETIC

One of the most successful and creative professors of homiletics, David Buttrick has devised a method based on his long experience of teaching, writing, and preaching.[4] Buttrick, like his contemporaries Eugene Lowry and Paul Scott Wilson, bases his system largely on the pioneering work of Fred Craddock, whom we have noted previously. What has been called the "new homiletic" emerged out of Craddock's deep questioning of previous (deductive) preaching tactics, commonly used in earlier times. As we have already seen, narrative unity would comprise much of the strategy that Craddock has in mind for the well-crafted homily. But there is more, much more, and Craddock intends to plumb that well in the preaching process. Much of what Craddock revisits was, of course, influenced by new developments in communication theory that recognized the pivotal role that congregations have in receiving a message—not passively, but actively. To this end, Craddock's aim, like that of his successors, is to engage the whole listener as a partner in interpreting the text. As far as the new homiletic is concerned, even well-organized, deductive sermons reach only a certain portion of the human subject. The goal of induction is full participation, especially through the imagination. Craddock's revisionist theory of inductive homiletics thrives on enlivening the imaginative powers of the hearer, allowing them to see what they had never dreamed before in the context of worship. The defensive motivations of the Samaritan woman at the well, for instance, become an occasion to probe that aspect of the Gospel more deeply and become more involved with the way in which John's Gospel invites us to participate in the Word. "The galleries of the mind are filled with images that have been hung there casually or deliberately by parents, writers, artists, teachers, speakers, and combinations of many forces....By means of images the preaching occasion will be a re-creation of the way life is experienced now held under the light of the gospel."[5]

David Buttrick's homiletic method is a well-designed, useful, and imaginative structure intended for the hearer's deepening faith commitment. Like all good methods for preaching, Buttrick wants us first to grasp the *overall intention of the biblical text; this textual trajectory will become translated in the dynamic operation of the homily itself.* Buttrick takes very seriously that the biblical text is "an event-in-time." Richard Eslinger explains Buttrick's method: "Biblical language is intentional; a pericope will want to function in the consciousness of the hearer in some way. Therefore, an interpreter is never finished with a text when a 'message' has been found. For Buttrick, the central question becomes, What does the passage want to do?"[6] The key to

Buttrick's thought lies precisely in our ability to understand the way in which the Word functions as an ongoing instrument of "consciousness transformation." If the preacher simply reduces the biblical text to a message or, even worse, a kind of therapeutic bromide for happy living, then we have failed to see *God-in-the-world*. That is what the biblical text is ultimately signifying: the living presence of God acting *now* among the Christian people. As Buttrick himself says, "Christ continues to speak to the church and through the church to the world....Preaching is Jesus Christ because it opens to us salvific new life and discloses the reality of God-toward-us."[7] Clearly, Buttrick wants the homily to be less about themes and more about an event; that is what the Word has come to do. In the language of *Fulfilled in Your Hearing*, then, the preacher, as mediator of meaning, "names grace" in our midst.

In order for the listener to hear the Word more deeply and to engage in the world of proclamation, Buttrick builds three homiletic plots culled from the way in which he sees biblical narrative functioning. First, plots that are in the "mode of immediacy" are drawn from the narrational features of biblical texts. The preacher discerns the theological field of the text and asks what it is trying to do for a contemporary listener. He will have to translate the text's intention into a contemporary idiom. Let's say, for instance, that the preacher is giving a homily on Matthew 25:31–46, in which Jesus talks about the corporal works of mercy. How would this passage form a contemporary parable in the consciousness of the listener, perhaps especially around the area of social justice and social sin? Second, in the "reflexive mode," plots for preaching in the mode of immediacy mirror the sequential plot development of the passage itself. The reflexive mode tends to reproduce the kind of text we might find, say, in the Book of Wisdom or the Pauline letters. It is up to the preacher to gather up the kind of language that would interface most usefully in the consciousness of the hearer. Third, the "mode of praxis" is more directly concerned with what we might call topical sermons: a given text might call us to action, based on the given historical reality in which we find ourselves. I remember when I was preaching the vigil mass on the feast of the Lord's Baptism some years ago. It also happened that at the same time, there was a special vote being taken in Congress for our participation in the Gulf War. Based on the feast and the readings that were proclaimed, I saw the occasion of a call to war on this particular day as an opportunity to preach about being a child of God and an ambassador of peace, like Our Lord himself. There will be times when the biblical texts need us to address more directly the human political situation that faces us, especially around justice and peace, right-to-life issues, capital punishment, as well as wars of aggression and unfair economic systems. These biblical texts face us with the experience of *re*-presenting God-with-us and the preacher's responsibility in shaping faith-consciousness. As preachers, we are *re*-presenting the scriptures in a modern idiom, revealing God in the world.

On a more practical level, I think that Buttrick's greatest contribution remains his development of what he calls "moves," blocks of material organized in the homily that "move" the homily along in a linear, plotted fashion. Ron Allen summarizes the way that these "moves" work:

> Each move consists of the following parts. It begins with a *statement*, that is, a clear indication of the content of the sermon. The preacher must make this statement in two to four short, direct sentences, each one making the same point, but in different words. The preacher then *develops* the statement by explaining it, usually in clear, analytical language. After the development, the preacher offers an *image* that pictures the point made in the move. The move ends with *closure*. Like the statement, the closure is made up of two to four short, direct sentences that make the same point. They summarize the point of the move.[8]

These moves are distinct units that operate independently but are interlocked with each other. Crucially, *each move contains only one idea*, so there is a system of unity *within* each of the moves. "The unity is established by the statement and restatement at the start and finish of the move...and within the framework of the move, there is only one developmental system organized as a personal, temporal memory."[9]

The following is the first move for a homily for the Thirty-third Sunday (A) of Ordinary Time:

[Statement] The parable of the talents anticipates a strange God comfortable with those who are shamelessly bold. [Development] God loves the reckless. God is at home with speed demons. Religious stereotypes may try to convince us that we are supposed to be meek and mild, biding our tongue and our time. We make our plaster saints smile but not speak. So it is hard for us to figure out this little mind-bending parable. To take five talents and trade with the entire amount like the first servant would be the modern equivalent of investing an entire life savings of more than a million dollars into a business nobody ever heard of. On the other hand, to secure one talent and bury it like the last servant, would presuppose a time-honored way of thwarting robbery. In antiquity, to bury money was the safest way to guard against theft, since no one would be held liable.

That sounds pretty good. Sounds prudent, you know, the queen of the virtues. Yet not only does Jesus find the reckless servant worthy of promotion, but the more careful man is thrown into the darkness. According to Jesus' admonition in today's parable, it is better to risk losing everything than to play it safe.

[Image] And so the meek and mild old woman answers the telephone one day to find out that she won ten thousand dollars in the lottery. She gets on a bus and goes to Atlantic City. She wants to spend it all, hoping she can double or triple her money so she can leave her grandchildren a nice nest egg of an inheritance for their school.

[Closure] God loves bold warrior-grandmothers. He is close to those who take risks, who spend it all, who go for the gusto. The servant with the ten-thousand talents threw caution to the wind and God loves that. [The last claim **rounds out** the move by echoing the first sentence and provides a tight symmetrical structure for closure.]

It should be clear enough that moves thrive on unity and clarity. For Buttrick, the collective consciousness of a congregation cannot absorb a scattered amount of material, but needs ordered progression in order to experience a shift in consciousness. Moreover, he has concretized each of the moves with a particular image that leaves the hearer with a visual imprint of each of the statements. In each move, the Christian assembly is invited to cocreate a portion of the homily with the preacher by imagining the process of ongoing narration.

The unity of the homily is further guaranteed in the overall shape of the Buttrick sermon, which links the moves together. Each of the statements can be knotted to each other and form a complete and logical thought. To line up the statements of each move sequentially, then, forms the skeleton of the plot structure. Buttrick's method is designed for sermons of about thirty to forty-five minutes, but when he taught at Saint Meinrad School of Theology, he worked to help students develop a homily with a reduced number of moves. Here is a homily that I preached for the Second Sunday of Advent (A):

WAITING INSIDE THE PROMISE

From the 1820s until the mid-1840s, America's greatest folk painter, Edward Hicks, produced a series of 62 remarkable paintings detailing the utopian vision present in chapter 11 of the Book of the Prophet Isaiah. These astonishing depictions have become familiar to us as *The Peaceable Kingdom*. Hicks, who was a Quaker preacher, disclosed a world so strikingly placid that some might be tempted to call his vision naive. In his most famous of the *Peaceable Kingdom* paintings, a lion dominates the center of the panel, surrounded by children dangling from the ear of a tiger, with lambs passively asleep on a lush green carpet lawn. This swirling festival of colors is something like a dream-vision of childhood, a merry-go-round in which a kingdom of cuddly, stuffed animals suddenly spring magically to life. Even more remarkable, far in the background a group of colonial settlers joins in an amicable conversation with some Native Americans. That indigenous people and white settlers must have struck postcolonial America as utterly preposterous in a climate when relations between the two groups were anything but peaceful.

A "peaceable kingdom" seems impossible, even as Isaiah's utopia, uttered in the midst of a tortured Israel, was now fragmenting and dissolving before his eyes. Isaiah had the audacity to preach a redemptive landscape when the Assyrians and Egyptians—the two greatest enemies of Israel—were assailing them from the left and the right. The end was, in fact, coming, and closing in fast, with close to fifty fortified cities eventually in ruins. Such a nightmare would literally tear Israel in half. Perhaps Isaiah himself stood on a hill from afar, watching the red night sky of Israel go up in flames.

Little did the Prophet know that the smoke from the ruins of those ancient cities would drift far into the twentieth and twenty-first centuries. There, the flames of injustice would be enkindled in the brutal trenches of No Man's Land in World War I, and only a few decades later, smolder in the death camps of Auschwitz or Buchenwald. The toxic smoke of the Holocaust would yet again divide the chosen people from the world of justice and life. Out of the almost 10 million Jews living in Europe before World War II, only one out of three would survive. A "peaceable kingdom"? A kingdom of justice? After seeing the appallingly grotesque photographs of the concentration camps, sociologist and philosopher Theodore Adorno once said that, after Auschwitz, all art is bogus and kitsch. The images from Auschwitz are haunting: the emaciated figures posing as human bodies, the lifeless faces, the sunken eyes looking through a barbed-wire fence. Any such recollection of a "peaceable kingdom" after the horrors of human extermination, or the atrocity of the atomic bomb, becomes a delusion. Naïve Isaiah. The Prophet dreams of a utopia that seems like a fantasy or a fairy tale.

Yet the Prophet is not offering us a solution but a divine promise. Left to our own devices, we will always make war, as the present condition in the Middle East makes painfully clear. The "peaceable kingdom" will be built not by our ingenuity, but by the testimony of God's Word. Kingdoms forged by the language of war bring destruction and treachery, but God's Word brings peace and justice—and the coming of redemption. "He shall strike the ruthless with the rod of his mouth, and with the breath of his lips he shall slay the wicked." That is what the Word of God does: it comes out to heal and to make whole. As the Book of Wisdom tells us, when the night was still, God's all-powerful Word leapt down from heaven. The Word is coming, John the Baptist tells us, and he will baptize with water and the Holy Spirit and with fire. That is the promise that God has made us. To view Hicks' *Peaceable Kingdom*, then, is to see, not a childlike landscape for fools, but a world remade in God's image through the power of the Word. The Word will transform and heal and make all things new. The Assyrians may have laid Israel to waste, but Jerusalem survives to this day. And so the old woman, a Jewish survivor of war-torn Poland, slowly but steadily places her prayer petition in the Wailing Wall of the Old City of Jerusalem. The coming of the Savior is nothing less than the movement of God's Word made visible, transforming us to new life, a new covenant of peace.

So we wait inside the promise. We keep vigil in memory of God's holy covenant. It is above all God's promise—not ours—for justice and peace, which no political machine or ideology can ever establish here on earth. There is no other way to celebrate the marvelously converting season of Advent except in vigil for God's future. "Be it done unto me according to your Word." The power of God's Word resides in the scriptures themselves, which Paul reminds us are for our instruction and our encouragement. By staying close to the scriptures, we cannot but recall God's saving work in the past and what is occurring among us even now. There is the prophetic hope, the apocalyptic promise, wrapped in a mantle of justice. God's plan will triumph even in the midst of darkness and death; a legacy will come from the stump of a tree called Jesse. To live inside the promise means we recognize that God can do a new thing, something that wars and those who devise them cannot even begin to imagine. John the Baptist recognized God's renewing love when he said that the God of Abraham could raise up children even from cold stones. In Advent, we eagerly join the Baptist in the wilderness of waiting for the One who is to come in the midst of our night. And when we are tempted to falter, we might challenge ourselves with the question that Fr. Ronald Rolheiser puts to the Christian community: "Do we still take our longings and emptiness to God in prayer or do we demand that life gives us, here and now, the full symphony?"[10] We choose instead to live this season not by full orchestral music but by the promise of hymns of vigil and waiting. So the Church this Advent is a peaceful, nonmilitant, love-swept army clothed in violet, made up of hands outstretched to heaven. We implore by candlelight and hover intrepidly over God's Word about to be made flesh. Singing songs of longing, as we cry, "O come, O come, Emmanuel, and ransom captive Israel"; that is what we are up to this Advent season: recognizing the legacy of the promise and longing of the Christ who will fulfill its destiny. Yes, we live inside the promise. As a gathered community in Christ, celebrating Eucharist with the Word proclaimed and the wondrous deeds of the Lord remembered, we await the only one who can at last bring the true Peaceable Kingdom.

Each of the initial (italicized) statements follows one another in a logical pattern, much like a plot outline. If we think of the focus of the homily as the assembly of these statements, then we have a unified text gathered around a single pearl, a silver thread that guides the hearer along a particular trajectory. When Buttrick's method is performed correctly, there is little chance for subject scatter and disunity in the text. The narration moves from beginning to end by way of a single pearl of great price.

EUGENE LOWRY'S NARRATIVE LOOP

Eugene Lowry wants to bring inductive homiletics precisely within the range of the classic Western narrative plot structure. Lowry intends to engage his congregation through the tension that is embedded in every good plot structure. So, unlike Buttrick, who designs his homiletic plots around the way in which the biblical passages are shaped, Lowry has a particular pattern into which the homily and, indeed, the biblical text itself conform. This narrative route will unfold like a typical plot, from conflict through complications to climax and resolution. Lowry believes that dealing with the needs of the Christian assembly requires that they listen to the core of the biblical passage at exactly the right *narrative* moment: the climax in the homiletic plot. So the biblical text itself becomes the kind of antidote to the tension that has been creeping up in the homily. As with Buttrick, Lowry's method is geared for the listener.

Lowry's homiletic plot has five points of departure: *Oops, Ugh, Aha, Whee,* and *Yeah.* Taken together, these have been termed the "Lowry Loop."

The first point of departure is *"Upsetting the equilibrium (Oops!)."* The congregation may be expecting a cheery little nosegay about the biblical readings, or a nice little pious observation. Instead, it has its applecart rocked by a conflict. The preacher usually brings to light something that does not make sense about the text or texts. Or it may be a cultural issue that is provoked by the texts, or a personal, internal conflict of the text and values clash. In any case, the task for the preacher is "to stir the pot."

The second point of departure is *"Analyzing the discrepancy (Ugh!)."* At this point, the homily teases out the conflict or bind that has been initiated in the first sequence. This is a rather crucial phase in which the tension is deliberately kept going. Lowry has said that it is not unusual for homilies to flounder at this particular juncture in his method because this *tension has not been extended or teased out enough*. Narratives thrive on tension, and if the discrepancy is not teased out but revealed, the trajectory is lost in the homily. Indeed, the experience of deflated tension would certainly parallel the world of many homilies that fail to keep the congregation engaged by ignoring the strategies of narrative momentum. The "ugh" in the homily must sketch out in theological and anthropological detail the realities inherent in the initial bind.

The third point is *"Disclosing the clue to the resolution (Aha!)."* At this level of the narrative we are engaged in the classical notion of a plot twist, a principle of reversal. According to Lowry, "It turns things upside down. In the visualized plot line shown, the radical change of direction is intended to suggest how the sermonic idea is turned inescapably by the clue; things can never be seen in the old way."[11] This stage is only a clue, but it is also an *aha* moment for the congregation.

The next point follows somewhat naturally from the *aha* moment: *"Experiencing the Gospel (Whee!)."* The biblical text(s) become the moment of revelation, as the preacher broadens the *aha* moment for the hearers. The preacher is very much like a detective who is now revealing the entire nature of the puzzle he has come to solve. He gives full voice to the clue in light of the Gospel. This climax moment has been reserved for the biblical text; it is the source of salvation. The congregation has literally awaited the word of God for solving the mystery.

Finally, the last point of departure, *"Anticipating the future (Yeah!),"* invites the congregation to answer the question, "So what?" This is a final stage that works toward new possibilities. Having experienced the Gospel more fully and deeply, we are now ready to take on a new challenge.

Lowry's narrative homiletic method is often suited to certain liturgical occasions that have become blasé, predictable experiences or regrettable perfunctory liturgies. The "upsetting of the equilibrium" at the beginning phase of the homily signals a wake-up call to those who have come to the Eucharist expecting a traditional reading of the readings, say, for Easter Sunday. The method is also effective for certain types of funeral homilies, particularly those that must deal with the anger and shock of the congregation about the loss of a loved one. Here is my example of one such homily based on the following texts for a funeral liturgy for an adult: *Revelation 21:1–5a, 6b–7* (seeing a new heaven and a new earth); *Psalm 116* (being saved by God and returned to rest); *Mark 15:33–39* and *16:1–6* ("My God, my God, why have you forsaken me?" and then the empty tomb).

JIM: THE FAITHFUL WITNESS

We should not be here. When I look out at the sea of familiar faces, all of those who loved Jim so much, all I can say is, "When is someone going to wake me up from this nightmare?" It is the experience deep down that we all must feel right now—anger, despair, and perhaps most of all: emptiness. There was someone who loved life to the full, who made us laugh and cry, and now all we can feel is absence. That had to be the experience of those disciples who went to the tomb that Easter morning. They went expecting to find Jesus. Some presence of him, anyway. They wanted to care for him, to anoint his shattered body and give it some dignity. And what they found was emptiness. Nothing but a young man telling them that all they had left of him was gone. Even a memory now seemed to have been taken away from them.

That tomb was empty, but it was nothing close to what Jesus himself had felt on the cross. There he was, after a long impossible torture, and still they jeered at him in his shame. There was Christ, alone and deserted by everyone, rejected by his friends, his relations, his closest disciples. And there he was, the Son of God, the Beloved, who now felt abandoned by God himself: "My God, My God, why have you forsaken me?" That is the cry of emptiness, of being completely alone. How could this have happened to Christ himself? It was not supposed to go this way. The healings, the reconciliations, the restorations to a new order: they were all suddenly part of the past, of some other life. The young man who no longer had demons; the blind Bartimaeus who now could see; the paralytic made whole: all of them seem to suggest that we were moving toward some greater end. At the very least, how could God allow his only Son to enter into this despair in which everything looked like an empty well in the middle of a forgotten desert? An empty tomb is matched only by the cries of Jesus himself, seemingly forsaken on the cross on a dark afternoon. God appears to be nowhere in sight.

I was getting pretty depressed about the way that God seems to let us down just when we need him the most, until I remembered a scene in the hospital with none other than Jim himself. I came last week and he was sitting up and telling the nurse not to worry about her son Dave, who had recently gotten into trouble. Jim was like that. Not only some of the time but all of the time. He knew the cancer was going to have its way with his body, but he told me that no disease would ever take away his relationship with God and his family. Far from being empty, Jim was about as full of love as I had ever seen him. He had more life in him on that hospital bed than most people have in a lifetime. He said, "Father, it's going to be alright. Death is not going to win this one. Christ is going to come and get me before the devil even knows I'm a goner." (Jim loved bringing a bit of Irish humor to almost everything, you know.) I told him that I knew that and I was sure he knew it too. "But," he said to me, asking me to stoop down so he could whisper in my ear, "just make sure my family and friends know it. They might forget about it. You know, this hospital stuff can be pretty overwhelming."

It was as if an alarm went off in my head, and I heard the young man in the empty tomb telling *me*, "Do not be amazed! You seek Jesus of Nazareth, the crucified. He has been raised; he is not here. Behold the place where they laid him." I had gone into that hospital room expecting to find the battered body of a friend, abused by cancer. Instead, I found the Good News preached by Jim himself. Yes, Jim was the homilist and the angel on his hospital bed even as he preaches now with me from this ambo. We might despair at his death, and God knows we need to grieve it, but he wanted to tell us that the Lord was coming to raise him up. Jim dying was not in that hospital bed; he was risen already! And it was then I knew that when Jesus cried out in anguish and rejection on the cross, his Father was close by him with a promise. It was a promise that the Faithful Witness would be vindicated and freed from the shackles of death. We are confronting a mystery, not emptiness. It is the cloud of grief that may blind us for now, but we know that when that fog dissipates, we will see the risen Christ, newly sprung from the tomb.

And so there is urgency to our task this morning—to tell the Good News and to comfort those who have been crushed by the loss of a husband, a father, a friend. We have been given a task by Jim himself to fill the void of what we think is empty. The Christian assembly has a special responsibility after this liturgy. We are witnesses to the resurrection. Not the kind of resurrection that is all about fireworks or soldiers fainting at the tomb. But the kind of resurrection that is born of faith. Faith is what Jim had buckets of. We all know that. His proclamation has got to make a difference in our lives because his life did. That was faith in action, which has now been passed on to us. Nobody is going to build a shrine for Jim at that hospital room, with its smell of antiseptics and starched linen. Jim has sent us out to seek the risen Lord. He has given us reason to vanquish despair from our lives. Even now he tells us of a God who has made all things new by his love. And so we see, like John the Evangelist, a new heaven and a new earth. This is a God who is close to the broken hearted and who comes to us even in emptiness. The darkness of the tomb will not prevail. And one day we will all say with Jim that refrain we know even now to be on our lips: "Praised be Jesus Christ, victor over sin and death."

Lowry has allowed the narrative process to be the occasion where the biblical passage finds its true goal—the ears of the hearers. This homiletic strategy places him very close to Fred Craddock, who urged the preacher to facilitate the biblical Word, "releasing" the power of the scriptures into the ears of the assembly. That plotted narrative homily is always at the service of the Word of God. These structures for preaching, needless to say, do not exist for themselves. Moreover, the congregation has been taken through a process of *inductive discovery* whereby the scriptures become the gifted solution in the faith journey. In the case of a funeral homily, it is not the words of the preacher that provide consolation, but the Gospel itself that salves those bitter wounds. The narrative process has taken the grieving congregation from anger into an exploration of faith. That should be reason enough to trust the inductive process in the homily. No amount of information dispensed during a homily, however well intentioned, can help a congregation grieve at a funeral for a loved one. The Gospel must be felt and struggled into the road to faith.

PAUL SCOTT WILSON'S FOUR PAGES

As I have already observed, facing the congregation with a moment of disequilibrium at the beginning of the homily is a fine inductive narrative strategy. With this homiletic plot in mind, Paul Scott Wilson has created a method that he refers to as the *four pages of the sermon*. Wilson is not suggesting that the sermon or homily be exactly four pages, or that the various movements he recommends should only fit on one page or the other. Rather, the device of "pages" is a useful metaphor to describe four quarters of the homily as a "way to do theology and to facilitate theological renewal in preaching."[12] Wilson recommends that each of the pages might be assigned to the days of the week, thereby providing reflection time for the preacher to mull over the biblical readings before preaching on the following Sunday. Not surprisingly, Wilson designed the Four Pages with a fundamental purpose in mind: to ensure sermon unity by having one text, one theme, one doctrine, one need, one image, and one mission all interface in the same sermon. Wilson's signposts are useful truth-tellers of homiletic unity. And if we forget them, Wilson offers an easy (if awkward) sentence: The Tiny Dog Now Is Mine. These signposts interface and provide a kind of checklist for the homily during and after preparation.

One Text

We may choose to weave in various strands of biblical texts from other readings in the Sunday Lectionary, but the homily should land on a single text; there simply is not enough time to cover all the texts adequately. The worst possible strategy is to go through a kind of inventory that is something like this: "In our first reading, in our second reading, then in the Gospel." That is an invitation to scattering. It is okay and, depending on the Lectionary readings, appropriate to bring in the other texts as supportive of the main scriptural reading, but it is a mistake to try to handle them all equally.

One Theme Statement

This is Wilson's version of Thomas Long's focus statement. It needs to be single, simple, and declarative, is never expressed as a question, and always deploys a strong, active verb. More often than not, God is the subject of the sentence; this helps to insure a theological focus to the theme statement. Moreover, as Wilson says, "A theme sentence will not stand as an adequate summary of the text; it is rather a clear marker of one path, amongst other possibilities, through what the preacher interprets to be the heart of the text."[13]

It should be noted that this statement is not a passage lifted from the readings and posed at the beginning of the homily as if the preacher were going to give a homily on this particular statement in the text. That strategy, common enough for some preachers, fails to allow the dynamics of the narrative to unfold. The biblical text then becomes reduced to a series of sayings or quaint pious apothegmata. Also, this theme is not the kind of thin, underdeveloped thematic that Untener also eschews, since the promise in Wilson's integrative schema is precisely to push the congregation deeper by asking them to hold a "single pearl."

One Doctrine

Cardinal William Levada cautions against immediately leaping from the scriptural readings to the needs of the people. He appropriately identifies the importance of doctrine in the homily when he speaks of preaching doctrinally as "a bridge" for the congregation.[14] For Catholic preachers, the *Catechism of the Catholic Church* is an enviable resource with which to partner with biblical text and theme statement. If, for example, the text is John 15 ("I am the vine, you are the branches"), the theme statement might be: "God never fails to provide for his people." The one doctrine might be a nourishing reflection on the Trinity and the indwelling of the Spirit speaking in the Church. Wilson himself also realizes the importance of theological reflection in the homily. Moreover, his point about doctrine concerns textual integration in the overall look of the homily: what doctrine best serves the theme sentence and the text. At the same time, this doctrinal aspect of Wilson's method insures what Levada calls "scriptural-based doctrinal homilies."[15]

One Need

This feature makes sure that the homily has a primal pastoral connection. Or to put this more bluntly: "So what?" Is this homily going to make any difference in the lives of the people in the pews? Wilson suggests that there are several ways of identifying the needs of the congregation. One is to return to the theme statement and ask: "What question does this answer in the life of a person or people in the church?"[16] And so, returning to our theme statement with John 15 (God never fails to provide for his people), we might imagine how this statement about God's unfailing love and nourishment becomes an answer to *these* people at *this* time. These are concrete, historical realities, not abstract principles. To allow the people of God a voice in asking such a question suggests a pastoral reality, not an idealistic wish on the part of the preacher. Another possibility for determining

the need of the congregation is to *return to the one doctrine* identified with text and theme statement. If the doctrine is the Holy
Trinity, we can say that these questions follow: "How is God
present in the world?...Where has God been living and active in
human history?...Where is God now?" Again, this is *one* need.
Undoubtedly, a given congregation will have as many needs as
there are people present in the Christian assembly.

One Image

In his discussion of images, Wilson is similar to Buttrick in
so far as he is suggesting that the use of images will always underline and concretize the point and thereby help the homily to jetti-
son lethal abstractions. That is not to say that the image avoids a
theological purpose. On the contrary, the very point of the image
is to engage the congregation not only in conceptual unity but
also in theological unity as well. "In the course of the sermon the
image should become theological; it ought to become united with
the theme statement and thereby become a visual and memory aid
for God's action."[17] In using images to create a theological connection, Wilson is in good company with the Evangelists themselves. In fact, John 15 already provides an image of the vine and
the branches and the One who tends them, an image that Christ
used appropriately for an agrarian culture in first-century
Palestine. Depending on the cultural context, the preacher will
want to discover another, more contemporary image that could
express a similar theological meaning embedded in John 15.

One Mission

The homily necessarily invites the Christian assembly to
move out and evangelize, much like the Eucharistic Liturgy itself.
By mission, Wilson is asking us to consider the single mission of
purpose that results from the one text, one theme, one doctrine,
one need, and one image. In reflecting on these signposts gleaned
from a prayerful homiletic reading of John 15, the invitation to

mission might be: "To live in the presence of God." Or, "to allow God's mysterious presence in Christ given at baptism to become a reality in our lives."

The signposts point to the importance of unity in the homily. Once these are aligned, it is possible to see the unfolding of the particulars of the Four Pages and the further dynamic that they add to the homiletic text. And indeed, the Four Pages that Wilson describes are just as useful as his signposts in shaping a homily. He creates four quadrants or fields of meaning through which the homily will move more broadly. These pages are indications of the way the homily is plotted.

Page One: Trouble in the Bible

This follows immediately from the introduction and deals with the "one text" that has been established. I find that this particular strategy is quite helpful for grappling with biblical texts that are often difficult to hear. One such notoriously dissonant biblical text is Genesis 22, the sacrifice of Isaac. We can count on the fact that most people will struggle with a God who asked Abraham to perform such a horrible, dreadful task. Delving into the trouble in that text would be fairly easy and run somewhat like this: God appears to be breaking his promise that Abraham would have descendants without number. Instead, the sacrifice of Isaac, his only son, would mean that there is no legacy of progeny. Sometimes it is harder to find trouble in other texts, but we need to keep digging for what might be hidden. If there is no problem, there is probably not much in the way of Good News either! As Wilson puts it, "The word that condemns also liberates. Our sin and brokenness is always in tension with the grace God freely gives to us."[18] The text does not have to be as baffling or as difficult as Genesis 22, but a matter to wrestle with, nevertheless.

Page Two: Trouble in the World

The trouble here is an extension of the previous page, but identified as a contemporary problem. We might recall that the preacher is called to name not only grace but the demons of the congregation as well. In keeping with Genesis 22, we might raise the issue of promise keeping and its failure in our contemporary society.

Page Three: God's Action in the Bible

At this point, we encounter the narrative twist, or the turn that we found in Lowry's "aha" moment in the homiletic plot. It is the time to see God's action in the Bible, a redemptive look at the Word. Therefore, we might think that the passage is about God breaking his promise, but it is really about Abraham's love and faith. How well will Abraham keep his promise of love for God? Far from the breaking of a divine promise, it is a passage about love and the flourishing of a relationship.

Page Four: God's Action in the World

Now we have an opportunity to see the way in which the biblical text is going to make a difference. God's action in the world becomes a new revelation to see the wonders of hope and redemption. So, based on our new insights about Abraham in Genesis 22, God transforms us by a new and deep relationship with him. Sometimes that is going to look very mysterious, and we may even still think that God is unfaithful. But in faith we remember our own promise and our covenant at baptism. We have a chance to give away what we think is most precious—our own self-interest. That is the Good News. It is an invitation to give away even the most precious thing we have in order to find life and love. In this page, the preacher names grace. Note that the action that is addressed here in Page Four needs to answer the problem posed in Page Two. If we are breaking our promises, the Gospel calls us to liberate ourselves from what binds us and to live in freedom.

What would Wilson's method look like when the signposts are integrated with the Four Pages? Here is a useful illustration, based on the raising of Lazarus (the Gospel for the Fifth Sunday of Lent, cycle A). A somewhat shortened version of a "Wilson homily" preached on this reading might look something like this:

WAITING FOR GOD

[Introduction] One of the greatest tests of friendship is loyalty. To be "true to the end" is about the best thing you can say about someone. I am always choked up when I think about people I have been friends with since grammar school. That is a long time to be able to say, "I remember when…" I saw two women at a restaurant recently. One of them had been crying and I overheard one of them say, "I'll be there for you." That is a great thing to see. Such friendship has been valued in literature over the years. When Patroclus is felled by Hector in the Iliad, Achilles takes revenge for the sake of his friend. In Shakespeare's *Romeo and Juliet*, Tybalt kills Mercutio, Romeo's best friend, but the star-crossed lover avenges his death. These are dramatic, life-or-death episodes, but they reveal the importance of loyal friendship. The surest condemnation in any wisdom literature is betrayal. "If I had to choose between betraying my friend and betraying my country," E. M. Forster once said, "I hope that I would have the guts to betray my country." Major failures in character are described as "He's just a good-time Charley," or "He is never there when you need him." These are the flaws of friendship, and they expose companionship's most important quality: loyalty. When a friend needs us, we come running.

[Page One] Jesus delays on his way to Jerusalem. [One text] I did not say words normally associated with Jesus. "Jesus healed." "Jesus cured." "Jesus changed water into wine." No, Jesus waited around and delayed. He had the opportunity to heal, but he didn't take it. This was no ordinary person that needed the Lord's attention, mind you. It was his close friend Lazarus, brother of his dear friends Mary and Martha. All of these folks seemed to be as close to a family as Jesus had during his lifetime. Last Sunday's Gospel found us in the midst of a powerful curing of a man born blind. But where was Jesus for Lazarus? There is no problem with distance here. Bethany was only two miles away. And to make matters even more inexplicable, the Gospel says that Jesus remained for two days where he was. Only then did he go back to Judea to see his sick friend. If I were sick, I would want someone to be with me as soon as possible. There is an urgency about being critically ill that requires immediate action. True friends drop everything and go to the bedside of the ones they love. They don't delay.

[Page Two] We delay too. We might talk a radical line about being there for people, but when are we going to come to the aid of those millions of people who are without health care? [One need] We often stall when it comes to doing good works. I remember a former monk telling me that he once went to a local emergency room in Florida with his brother and sister-in-law. The woman was experiencing severe abdominal pains. They waited for five hours in the emergency room before they were even seen. One of the more-or-less guileless nurses expressed surprise when the monk's brother produced a health insurance card. "Oh, sorry we kept you waiting; we thought you were on welfare." Astonishing what we do to one another, isn't it? When was the last time anyone ran to the aid of a noble cause instead of watching television? We claim to be against the death penalty, but more often than not we are just waiting around while the death watch continues in prisons across America. Back in the sixties, protest was a way of life because lives were being lost in Southeast Asia. We hear occasionally about this or that protest about the war in Iraq. But it is too late, isn't it? We should have been wearing our black armbands and marching, immediately after the Bush administration clamored for war and Congress endorsed it. But we delay. We'd prefer to watch reality TV, to spend time with stories about Britney Spears, or to wait with our popcorn and see who the next American Idol is going to turn out to be.

[**Page Three**] Fortunately, God does not wait for long and for reasons only God knows. [**One theme**] Jesus delayed for a purpose: it was not to cure illness that he came but to reveal God's glory. I wonder what he was doing during those two days he spent delaying. We can bet that he spent most of that time in prayer. Jesus was probably experiencing the reality of his true mission: to be the image of God's glory in the world. He did not come to be the doctor of the body, but the redeemer of human kind. That is what Jesus tried to convince Martha about. She thought that if he had not delayed, Lazarus would not have died. But that was never the point. [**One doctrine**] Christ came to reveal the resurrection as a moment of new creation, the glory of God. As St. Irenaeus said in a treatise against heretics, "The glory of God is the human person fully alive." That is what is revealed in the Good News as this drama unfolds in Bethany. The glory of God is the compassion revealed in the death of a friend: "Jesus wept." How powerful those words are: The Son, the revealed Word of the Father abiding in the Spirit, is unfolding for us. This is a trinitarian moment in John's Gospel. The Father's glory is hidden in tears. This is the divine compassion that is liberating, freeing. It is the compassion that says, "Roll away the stone....Unbind him." That is the liberating voice of the Lord who suffers with us. In a certain sense, this passage in John is a real prelude to the passion of the Lord. Compassion is the foreshadow of passion. We will see the glory of God revealed again in the passion of Christ and in his resurrection. Like a true and trusted friend, Jesus will come and get us in the darkness of the tomb. [**One image**] He is like a rescuer in search of someone who has fallen from a mountaintop. He goes down deep into the valley looking for the lost climber and will not return until he has his friend in his arms. This is where the Good Shepherd becomes our best friend. He descended into the darkness of death and went to the underworld, to retrieve not a lost sheep, but his friends. And he never delayed for an instant to free those enslaved by death. Jesus went after Lazarus and retrieved him from the depths of the tomb.

[**Page Four**] We know we can be confident in God. There is no getting around it: illness and death will be with us as long as we are on this earth. We cannot pretend that they will go away. Or that we will be able to find a miracle cure for terminal illnesses tomorrow. Suffering and death are the sad realities of the human condition. We will sometimes feel terribly alone. But our hope in the resurrection is made real by Jesus himself, who is the resurrection and the life. He will not abandon his friends to corruption. He is the *Logos*, the Word, who with the Father made the world and those who dwell in it. He will not abandon us to a smelly grave. A dark tomb. A place bereft of his presence. God is *for* us. The Spirit dwells *in* us, as Paul reminds the Romans. That Spirit does not know corruption. Imagine Jesus having to face his close friend's death, and even his own. No wonder he grieved. Death must have seemed so foreign to him, so alien to who he was. The one who came to redeem was a stranger to corruption. When he wept for Lazarus, he was also weeping for us, his friends—weeping because of the tragedy of sin and the gift of life. That compassion was bound to set us free from corruption and the sting of death.

[**Conclusion**] Our savior is about to take our hand, bring us up out of the valley of death, and take us to safety. With friendship we grasp his hand, knowing that he will be with us as the resurrection and the life forever. We now go out to live the resurrection with confidence. We can say to prisoners: Come out without delay. The Lord has set you free from your bonds. What are the things that bind you? Jesus will untie you. And the last thing to be untied will be death. He will come to deliver his friends. [**One mission**] With that confidence he sends us forth from our tombs of hesitation: fear to love, fear to act, fear to bring others out from what binds them.

PRACTICAL SUGGESTIONS FOR BEGINNING AND ENDING ANY HOMILY

To my way of thinking, the most important thing about introductions is also the most obvious: *They should introduce the first stage of the homily*. Introductions are not "warm-up acts" or "getting acquainted with the preacher" sessions. They are tight, well-organized systems that strategize to gather the congregation with language so as to lead them into the first stage of the homily. It is easy to overlook this very crucial aspect: *Introductions are there for a purpose.*

Wilson suggests six ways of handling introductions[19]—which work well for all homiletic methods and without resorting to the tired standard opening of a joke, which often has no relation at all to the readings.

✔ Use variety.

- *Start with a story* that suggests the *flip* side of the theme sentence or the God-action statement.

- *Start with a not-too-serious experience* of the general theme—but neither a joke, nor something unrelated to the theme. A not-too-serious experience is a way of giving folks who are not necessarily ready for a heavy theme some time to be eased into it.

- *Start with a social justice issue.*

- *Start with a news item,* for example, on recent statistics about divorce or infidelity, in keeping with the flip side of the theme statement. Generally speaking, however, we need to be attentive to the kind of impact that some news items will have on impressionable congregants. The homily above uses not exactly newsy items, but gleans from anecdotal information and surveys world literature.

- *Start with a fictional account.* This can be a story that leads right into the biblical text.

- *Start with the introduction conflated with the First Page* ("Trouble in the Text").[20]

✔ Write the introduction later.

Writing introductions is not easy and usually should be left until the body of the homily is at least somewhat sketched out. How else do we know what to introduce? Economy should be the guiding principle for all homilies, and that is especially true when it comes to introductions. If these early sentences are wordy and disorganized, the congregation is signaled that the rest of the text will follow in similar fashion.

Where introductions open a window onto the first stage of the homily, conclusions beg to bring closure to the text. Many good homilies have been ruined because the preacher either did not know how to land the plane or had several false landings. The good homily is like bringing a flight home with all the passengers safe and sound, ready to deplane.

Here, too, Wilson suggests six ways to conclude a homily. A summary of his six ways basically says—

✔ Return home but at a different and hopefully higher point.

- *Return to a story or use a new story.* The preacher could come back to the story of Lazarus or develop a new one.

- *Return to the doctrine.* That is the strategy of the homily above in which the resurrection is revealed by Christ.

- *Return to the dominant image.* The homily would restate it as a visualization of the theme statement. The mountain rescuer comes to claim us from death.

- *Return to congregational needs.* We will be fortified by our assurance that God is with us and given the strength to act.

- *Return to mission.* We are sent forth to liberate others from what binds them.

- *Return to the cross and resurrection.* We could have brought in Paul's Letter to the Romans (the second reading) here in relationship to the cross and resurrection, to which we turn again and again.

No matter what kind of homiletic method you might find useful, it is worth trying Wilson in order see the way that his paradigm functions rhetorically. Wilson's suggestions can be adapted rather easily. Furthermore, his advice for introductions and conclusions makes sense even if one does not adhere to the Four Pages method precisely and exactly. In general, we need to pay close attention to methods because they are vehicles for the hearer, structures that enable our messages, fueled by our encounter with the Word, to take shape. Even when modified, these inductive practices—armatures for the homily—will only enable better preaching and listening.

MISSTEPS

✕ *Thinking that the homily is only about content will always be a false move.*

That assumption is problematic in a number of ways. First, a bias toward content presumes that the Christian assembly comes to the liturgy only for information. Most do not. In any case, the Eucharistic Liturgy is an act of worship, praise, and thanksgiving, offered to God through the Eternal Word, the Son, Christ Jesus. Those baptized in Christ come to have their faith deepened, which undoubtedly will involve, at some level, the content of the homily. But the way they embrace that substance should *induce* a faith experience rather than *deduce* a conclusion about a proposition.

The second fault with the assumption that the homily is only about content presumes that the form or the vehicle that carries the message is of little importance. Every good poet starts writing the most demanding of poetic forms, observing strict formal rules of meter and rhyme, so that he or she learns how to create a poetic environment for the sake of the reader, as well as enhance poetic skill. Robert Frost used to say that such restrictions are crucial for effective poetry. "Writing in free verse is like playing tennis with the net down." The homiletic method provides the net and the rules of the game.

✗ *Missing the dynamics of narrational preaching usually follows from ignoring form.*

Sensing what happens in narrative and its essential operations is crucial to understanding the way in which the homily will unfold to the hearer. The three methods described by Buttrick, are avenues into Lowry, and Wilson inductive preaching that *allow the congregation to own the homiletic process more fully.* If narrative is not understood as a process driven by plot and unpacked by the collective mind during the homily, then the inductive strategy will fail.

QUESTIONS AND PROJECTS FOR CLASS

1. Have the students select a homiletic method (Buttrick, Lowry, or Wilson) and allow them to preach using these strategies. Discuss in class what worked and what did not.

2. Ask each student to select a different parable from the Gospel of Luke. In a class discussion, consider its narrative method. What are the plots of the parables? How would the students retell these parables in contemporary language?

3. Assign students to write a collective homily in which each person would take a different component of Lowry's stages of the homiletic plot (Oops! Ugh! Aha! Whee! Yeah!). How does the homily hold together?

QUESTIONS FOR REFLECTION

1. What kind of homiletic method do I currently use? If I do not use one, what is keeping me from experimenting with this process?

2. Consider the homilies you have heard over the years. What are the ones that have moved you deeply? Why?

3. How do you understand biblical narrative? Do you pray with the scriptures with an ear toward preaching the text? If not, the next time you meditate on the scripture, ask yourself: "Will this preach?"

Step Five

COMMUNICATING IN
CONTEMPORARY CULTURE

Here's my theory of motivation: If you grab someone
by the ear and take off running, their body generally
follows.
—Kerry Patterson et al., *Crucial Confrontations*[1]

The rise of the new homiletic in the early 1970s was a
wake-up call, not only to an innovative process of preaching, but
also to a revolution in human learning that had been underway
for almost a century. Craddock and others were signaling what
was already a fact: that American culture was shaped around the
hearer—or more precisely, the *spectator*. It is not an exaggeration to say that mass culture in the twentieth century had turned
Americans into *receivers*. In order to see the rise of the influence
of the audience, we need look no further than the nascent film
industry at the end of the nineteenth century, as nickelodeons
were both transforming and being transformed by the astonishing influx of immigrants into the United States. Indeed, today we
are a nation of receivers—from radio, film, television, Internet—
a nation that has become educated, irrevocably, by induction.[2]
That the nation has become receivers is not quite the same as
saying we became passive; on the contrary, most theorists insist
that education is best communicated through a transactional

interaction that urged the viewer or hearer to engage the message more actively. Communication is the province of the receiver. J. Randall Nichols puts this change in terms of preaching: "Although much of traditional homiletics focuses on the preacher's work in constructing a sermon, a communication approach recognizes that communication is an inherently constructive process in which the receiver of messages actively builds meaning on the basis of information at hand, both from signals provided by the sender and from existing or ambient information in the receiver's field."[3]

The question that preachers face today, then, is not whether to preach inductively, but rather, what kind of inductive process now suits the contemporary idiom and which form best engages the active faith experience of the hearer? We have already seen what such a process might look like with a homiletic method in Step Four, but communication is ongoing and always mutating. For example, there was a time in which sitcoms dominated the major networks, but now that format has been greatly reduced by competition from other formats on cable television, and the rise of other subgenres deploying much more audience interaction, such as *American Idol.* Canned laughter used to supply an imaginary community for those watching sitcoms; now the U.S. audience creates their own interactive community by inviting friends over for an evening with reality TV. That shift in format tells us something, not only about audience taste, but also about how folks engage and are engaged by mass culture.

These insights into popular culture are vital clues for the preacher. It is well to note, then, that the preacher proceeds onto Step Five without a map: communicating with contemporary culture will be determined precisely by the changing circumstances of both the global and local community. The goal in Step Five is not to imitate the mass cultural text but *to learn from its strategy.* Indeed, the preacher's guide on this step is Jesus' admonition to be aware of "the signs of the times." Church documents promulgated from the time of Paul VI through John Paul II have greatly emphasized the utilization of mass media for the work of spreading the Gospel. Paul VI's apostolic exhortation "On Evangelization in the Modern World" puts it dramatically: "The Church would feel guilty before the Lord if she did not utilize these powerful means that human skill is daily rendering more perfect."[4] And John Paul II made it clear that a new evangelization will be effective only if the Church learns from modern communication methods as well as the culture from which it has emerged.

> For the new evangelization to be effective, it is essential to have a deep understanding of the culture of our time in which the social communications media are most influential. Therefore, knowledge and use of the media, whether the more traditional forms or those which technology has produced in recent times, is indispensable. Contemporary reality demands a capacity to learn the language, nature and characteristics of mass media.[5]

SO LITTLE TIME: TV COMMERCIALS AND COMMUNICATION

If we really want to understand the way in which Americans learn by induction and develop preaching strategies accordingly, then our first stop ought to be advertising. Sounds strange, doesn't it, a preacher turning to television ads for advice? Yet, St. Augustine had some very pointed things to say about preachers availing themselves of contemporary rhetoric:

> So since facilities are available for learning to speak well, which is of the greatest value in leading people either along straight or along crooked ways, why should good men not study to acquire the art, so that it may fight for the truth, if bad men can prostitute it to the winning of their vain and misguided cases in the service of iniquity and error?[6]

Needless to point out, I am not trying to say something either good or bad about the nature of advertising or the Church's potentially antagonistic relationship to Madison Avenue. My suggestions throughout these steps have been to operate within a nexus of a cultural dialectic, providing insights for the future of a Catholic homiletic and a new springtime for evangelization. Once again, I take my cue from the scriptures and the Church itself. Paul tells the Corinthians, "I have become all things to all people, that I might by all means save some. I do it all for the sake of the gospel, so that I may share in its blessings" (1 Cor 9:22–23). As the Pontifical Council for Culture observed in *Toward a Pastoral Approach to Culture*, "the influence of the media which has no frontiers, especially as regards advertising," asks Christians to be very attentive to the way in which an enormous amount of people are being formed by television.[7] Although my efforts are meant to surface only a few useful ideas and to remain somewhat speculative, I think we can say for our purposes here that advertising specializes in the rhetoric of *communicating in a field of relationships* in order to get the viewer to purchase a particular product.

The rhetoric of advertising represents the most persuasive form of argument in our culture: it is the platform on which commodity culture survives or falls. Television advertisements are particularly useful forms for preachers to understand because these "spots" are compressed (usually to thirty seconds) and are fiercely economic tools used to get on the wavelength of the contemporary hearer. To study the rhetoric of television commercials, even limited and very briefly, showcases how the spectator becomes part of an interpretive community worth attending to. The preacher needs to be aware of contemporary advertising, not only in order to know what competition he is facing on Sunday—engaging a congregation that has spent as much as six hours a day or more watching television—but also as a tool in shaping the language of the homily. These are what Augustine might have called the available "facilities for speaking well." I see an understanding of modern culture as the continual involvement of the Church with dialogue. And so preachers must ask: What is the contemporary idiom of our culture and how can I best communicate with my people the message of the Gospel of Jesus Christ?

Together with Dr. Richard Stern, my colleague at St. Meinrad School of Theology, I routinely show the now-classic commercials of Joe Sedelmaier to the students in the Introduction to Homiletics class. Sedelmaier was a former art director at J. Walter Thompson and Young and Rubicam, who developed a new way of understanding television commercials, mostly by changing our expectations with casting and stylistics. His most recognizable commercial was for Wendy's "Where's the beef?" Coincidentally, Sedelmaier began his innovative thinking in the world of advertising roughly around the same time that the new homiletic was underway as well. Sedelmaier's influence has been felt in our own day in the world of advertising and beyond, and so a useful analysis of a few of his commercials would be profitable for the preacher on Step Five.

Consider, if you will, another Sedelmaier spot for Wendy's, a campaign that was launched in 1984 and became a celebrated success. Like many of Sedelmaier's strategies, the Wendy's television ads are miniature plots waiting to unravel, mysteries longing to be disentangled. That description may sound odd for a short commercial on television, but once again, narrative and the process of induction reach out to the audience to cause it to solve a problem posed, however tiny the time slot. And the problem to be deciphered, or the answer begging to be resolved, will be delivered by the product itself, in this case, Wendy's. One Wendy's commercial, this one called "Processed Chicken," begins with a small line at a fast-food counter. A nerdy little man looks discontentedly at the content of his box of food. Another man stands waiting to be served when a voice-over says, "Some hamburger places actually serve processed chicken." The man waiting to order at the counter observes the man ahead of him and says, "Excuse me, but what was that in there?" "Chicken?" says the nerd. "Processed?" asks the other man. The server goes on to answer: "That is when they take a lot of chicken and assemble its respective parts....And I hear tell that all parts are crammed into one big part and then the one big part is cut into little parts and parts is parts." The narrator says finally, "You want something better. You're Wendy's kind of people." Throughout this hyperactivity—accentuated by the carnival-esque accordion music in the background and rapid-fire dia-logue—extreme close-ups are intercut of juicy Wendy's chicken with accompanying description of the chicken that is certainly not processed. Needless to say, Wendy's chicken is the solution to the problem of processed chicken and we figure it out.

Many of Sedelmaier's ads follow much the same narrative bend: There is a problem and then there is a solution that the viewer decodes and processes. A FedEx ad describes workers in peril because they forgot to send an important package, but their problem could have been solved if they had *only* used FedEx. People all across the country who are sick of their coffee (and, hilariously, throwing their coffeepots out the window by the hundreds so that they land on a meek postal worker) could solve their problem if *only* they would buy Mr. Coffee. The device is clear and direct, well plotted and economical. The tactic is repeated in countless other ads, probably less effectively than Sedelmaier's. Technology has added a further dimension to Sedelmaier's plot. In a 2008 FedEx spot (not Sedelmaier's) that aired on Superbowl Sunday, an employee informs his boss that he has found a solution to sending packages: giant carrier pigeons. The birds fly everywhere and pick up cars in the street, one of which crashes through the office window. "Let's switch to FedEx," the boss says. This is a slightly more absurd situation than the earlier Sedelmaier spot, to be sure, but the plot is the same. All these are miniature narratives drawing the audience into the tense world of a problem that requires a solution.

Sedelmaier deploys very eccentric characters as part of his tactic as well. In typical television ads, we expect stereotypes and stock characters; we don't expect a little old lady (actress Clara Peller) to petulantly ask, "Where's the beef?" More often than not, the characters appear to be mousy little men or old ladies, the antithesis of the Madison Avenue type for product associations. *But it is the surprise to our expectations that hooks us into the product.* Similarly, Sedelmaier's direction technique is also quite different from the conventional camera style as well. Sedelmaier typically shoots his characters at a straight angle shot, looking into the camera. The feeling the viewer gets is one of both intimacy and absurdity: intimacy because we are partnering with the character, so to speak, in a kind of subjective interaction; and absurdity, because the characters themselves are often offbeat and even goofy. They look like a joke that we have been allowed to share with a community of other viewers.

There is a grammar of sorts that we might be able to derive for preaching from Sedelmaier involving plots, unpredictability, and subjectivity. I have already suggested that plotting the homily is crucial to its function as a text that engages the listener, but here we see how rapidly the plot might both engage the spectator and solve a problem. The tension that is created at the beginning of the commercial suggests discontentment with the run-of-the-mill product, the status quo. The solution is the product: *Bingo!*

Similarly, we might ask: What are we doing at the beginning of the homily to prepare for a solution? If the People of God wait upon the Word at the liturgy, then, is the preacher creating a narrative of anticipation that will answer their hungers? Are we creating enough tension by recognizing and naming the problems that are ready to be devoured by the mysterious and consoling Word of God? The narrative tension that is created inside the homiletic text acknowledges our hunger for the Word of God in community. This process of narrative tension and release is exactly the process that Craddock, Buttrick, Lowry, and Wilson have been emphasizing in homiletic methods. Although Sedelmaier obviously does not operate in an ecclesial space with his television commercials, he has a way of gathering his audience so that we recognize cultural images together with a community of like-minded learners. He creates a broadcast community, a forerunner of the virtual community now standard fare in Internet usage. In the end, Wendy's is sold to a community, not just to an individual: "You're Wendy's kind of people." If we buy Wendy's, we will belong to those who recognize the flaws of those who sell processed chicken and come over to the Wendy's family. If that is not a secular conversion, I don't know what is. And all that in thirty seconds!

We need to recognize that unpredictability and even undaunted surprise are also ways into fine homiletic tactics. We should be deepening the faith of the congregation, not by manipulating them to buy things, but by pushing the envelope of traditional expectations. Succeeding in the area of unpredictability can mean the difference between a mediocre homily and a very good one, between keeping the hearer on the same level of faith and exciting them to move out into mission. Jesus' parables work precisely to refashion our expectations. In fact, parables function to tease us into new meaning. No wonder Jesus tells the disciples in Mark's Gospel that the reason he speaks in parables to the people is so that "they may indeed look, but not perceive, and may indeed listen, but not understand; so that they may not turn again and be forgiven" (4:12). What can Jesus mean by this except that he wants those to hear the parables to keep searching for meaning? Here is the Word thwarting expectations and allowing the seed of the Gospel to sink deep into rich soil where it will flourish. The Kingdom of God is like nothing we ever imagined. So, let's envision it like something we have never dreamed of before. We (re)grow the meaning of our (re)defined expectations because the Word has astonished us. Does the homily take the baptized assembly to a place where they did not expect to go so that they can be renewed with living water for their parched ground? Jesus offers his disciples an almost-but-not-yet vision of what might be. "Give me a drink," he tells the Samaritan woman at the well, as if to goad her into a yearning for the only thing that will satisfy her thirst. Similarly, we yearn for our own thirst to be quenched as well by the Word, spoken in scriptural-doctrinal preaching that satisfies the deepest needs of faith.[8]

Finally, Sedelmaier's ads tamper with stylistic conventions in camera work, an area that received some significant experimentation in the European film industry, especially in the late 1950s and 1960s. With some rare exceptions, Hollywood has never really changed much with its narrative story-telling techniques and has managed to maintain a conservative edge to feature films over the years. Americans know what to expect from a Hollywood movie and the television commercials that inform them. It is well known that one of the guiding principles of the film stylistics in this country is that there is a "fourth wall" that allows the viewers a kind of privileged point of view, watching the action unfold but not drawn into the screen action. (That principle does not apply globally, especially with Japanese directors like Yasuriro Ozu, who filmed at straight-angle shots rather than shot/reverse-shot angles.) Sedelmaier has picked up on this surprising feature in his commercials and used it to his advantage, causing the viewer to shift his or her point of view. In Sedelmaier's typical commercial, for instance, there are many straight angle shots that involve the viewer immediately in the screen action. We are not distant spectators but actors in the scene with the FedEx characters or the Wendy's hamburger servers.

How does this particular formal element in film stylistics play itself out in the homily—that is, in terms of encountering a character's feelings and actions more personally and directly? In most homilies, the preacher tends to approach the Gospel from outside rather than inside the text. Talking about the readings on Sunday often means that the homily devolves into some kind of commentary on the readings in the *Sunday Lectionary*, rather than an experience of what *Fulfilled in Your Hearing* refers to as speaking "through" the scriptures instead of "on" them. Or the homily could turn into some kind of naïve analogy of the scriptural text with everyday life. These homiletic tactics hardly push the congregation further into a deeper faith-experience or allow them to participate in the real challenge of the Gospel: the astonishment of the Kingdom that is upon us now. But consider the following question: Based on our insights from commercial television stylistics and communication, instead of taking a kind of authoritarian or objective role in preaching, can we tease out "subjective" character elements in the Gospel? The disciples certainly had their own point of view when they ascended Mount Tabor with Jesus. Subjectivity allows us a point of view that is fresh and that draws the congregation closer to the experience of the biblical witness. Can we imagine the reactions of Peter, James, and John to their experience of the Transfigured Lord? What would it be like to hear the experience of Mary of Bethany when she used costly ointment on the feet of Jesus and wiped them with her hair? *Imagining her perspective on the scene grants us a special insight into the Gospel.*

I hasten to add that, by suggesting a "subjective stance" with a particular character, I am not recommending either a relativist or a subjective interpretation of the Gospel. Far from it. I am simply asking the preacher to begin to attend to the *use* of an appropriate *form*, a kind of rhetorical container for the Gospel interpreted by the preacher. *Again, how we interpret the text and offer an exegesis to the congregation will largely determine what kind of form we should choose.* I will have more to say about this subjective quality of the homily later, when we look at how to engage a larger, multicultural dynamic. But suffice it to say at this point that, if mass culture engages its audience in effective ways by unexpected shifts in narration, from time to time the homily could benefit from an awareness of these rhetorical strategies. That insight, I believe, could lead the congregation into a new world, a place that can open up the possibility of the Word of God living in their midst.

MAKING THE GOSPEL STICK

The way in which the preacher absorbs the Word of God in a graced context and then sows the seed in hearers will vary according to cultural norms. Attending to popular culture, as I have suggested above, remains a way of reading the manner in which the historically formed congregation understands the process of induction anywhere from ten-second commercials to Hollywood feature films. I have suggested only a miniscule sample of a lively dynamic in broadcast media from which to draw in the homiletic process. As these avenues of mass communication unwind, you might consider what effect these aspects of popular culture are having on the congregation at large. Surely, the introduction of the Internet and the more extensive use of home computers have caused folks to process information differently from the way they did even ten years ago. Teenagers and young adults now cannot imagine life without a computer and live in virtual communities like MySpace, Facebook, and Twitter. They are thinking "into" machines. Machines are their partners for most of the day, either for school work or recreation. If we are to evangelize the modern world, then we need to understand in context the tools of communication as they arise. Even the questions we are currently asking today are antiquated tomorrow; today's technology is already outdated.

Thinking beyond mass culture to the world of business, preachers might discover dynamic colleagues with whom to dialogue. My colleague Dr. Rick Stern in the homiletics department at St. Meinrad School of Theology and Seminary is a regular subscriber to *Business Week* and often calls its bestseller list to my attention. In fact, when Dr. Stern teaches a class on Special Topics in Homiletics, he often turns to what the business community is busy reading these days. That bibliography might sound a world away from such church fathers as Origen or Leo the Great, or the classic writers of what used to be called *sacred oratory*. Those ancient commentaries will continue to be useful to preaching and provide a wealth of insight to interpretation. But how to deliver that message? We know now that it takes more to make an idea stick than even the best pious intention. So this is very much an eclectic course of action: Students should study the great religious classics, but they should also know how contemporary communication thrives and reinvents itself from year to year. To be wise as serpents and simple as doves could not be better advice for preachers who are attentive to the ways of rhetoric but also radically open to God's Word in prayer.

Recently, Chip Heath and Dan Heath, two brothers engaged in communication studies and strategies, have developed a best-selling resource devoted to understanding why certain messages survive and some do not. *Made to Stick: Why Some Ideas Survive and Others Die* is an exploration into the ways in which messages are received, recorded, and remembered. The Heath brothers' pondering of what makes things stick recalls our own discussion here into homiletics: sometimes we just don't ask whether people are getting it or not. *Made to Stick* pays attention to what folks think:

> Given the importance of making ideas stick, it's surprising how little attention is paid to the subject. When we get advice on communicating, it often concerns our delivery: "Stand up straight, make eye contact, use appropriate hand gestures. Practice, practice, practice (but don't sound canned)." Sometimes we get advice about structure: "Tell 'em what you're going to tell 'em. Tell 'em, then tell 'em what you told 'em." Or "start by getting their attention—tell a joke or a story."[9]

It is interesting to note a few things about this statement. Much of what the Heath brothers observe about an outdated way of "communicating" concerns the speaker and not the hearer. Sound familiar? Those bromides that favor the speaker over the hearer are still being shuffled and dished up to seminary students of homiletics in every denomination. Well into the 1960s, those who took any kind of public-speaking course related to writing sermons would have heard the familiar admonition above: "Tell 'em what you're going to tell 'em. Tell 'em, then tell 'em what you told 'em." Clearly, the hearer plays no role at all in this configuration. It is troubling enough when secular communication fails to avail itself to the audience, but when preachers do not acknowledge the viability of the baptized assembly as hearers of the Word, how can we say that a preaching event has occurred, or that the "full and active participation" of the People of God has been engaged in the whole liturgy. If Word has not been heard, then there has been no preaching. As *Fulfilled in Your Hearing* reminds us, "What is communicated is not what is said, but it is what is heard, and what is heard is determined in large measure by what the hearer needs or wants to hear."[10]

To put this vital relationship with the hearer another way and in the terminology of the Heath brothers, when public speaking was taught, the message was not made to stick. Writing for a business audience, on the other hand, the authors have narrowed their advice about "sticky" messages down to six points of departure: Simple, Unexpected, Concrete, Credible, Emotional, Stories (SUCCESs). As I will now suggest, these points are a nice roadmap for understanding the contemporary homily and echo much of what we have already seen in previous steps on the Ladder of Preaching. Throughout this section, I will make practical parallels between *Made to Stick* and the liturgical homily.

PRACTICAL SUGGESTIONS FOR MAKING THE HOMILY STICK

✔ Be Simple

By now simplicity and its importance in communicating an idea should not strike us as unfamiliar. The focus statement, which Thomas Long emphasizes as a key starting point for good homilies, is a matter of establishing the bare-bones message. So, too, the Heath brothers: "To strip an idea down to its core, we must be masters of exclusion. We must relentlessly prioritize....We must create ideas that are both simple *and* profound."[11]

Understanding simplicity will enable the preacher to appreciate the urgency of economy and why less is more. As we have seen earlier, there may well be five very interesting points in the homily, but the congregation will come away remembering none of them. The Heath brothers use the newspaper term *lead*, the beginning of a news story that has been utterly economized except for its essential point. "News reporters are taught to start their stories with the most important information. The first sentence, called the lead, contains the most essential elements of the story."[12] But getting to that essential core or focus of the homily may paralyze the writer with too many options. The one who communicates the message must be consistently aware that he or she prioritizes in the story. Journalists face the problem of "burying" the lead, perhaps in much the same way that preachers lose sight of their focus and loop in and out of extraneous material. After all, the preacher, like the journalist, is beset by things that need to be said, interesting things undoubtedly. But when it comes to simplicity, everything must work toward the lead. "Avoid burying the lead. Don't start with something interesting but irrelevant in hopes of entertaining the audience. Instead work to make the core message itself more interesting."[13]

Indeed, *the process of making the lead more interesting might also be called the "pearl"* in Ken Untener's terms, as we discussed earlier. That means the focus becomes deeper in the hearts of the congregation—much different from burying the pearl! Our task is to unearth the pearl of great price, not hide it.

Made to Stick wisely advises against turning our focus statements into sound bites. The key to simplicity is core *plus* compact. Compact alone is not enough. The ideal is "*short sentences (compact) drawn from long experience (core).*"[14] That is why the proverb and not the sound bite is the "Holy Grail" of simplicity. "A bird in the hand is worth two in the bush" is a core value that finds expression in a compact idea.[15]

THE HOMILY AND "SIMPLE"

The best way to see simplicity in action is to experiment with keeping daily homilies to ONE PAGE ONLY. I am well aware that hardly anyone even writes down daily homilies; that is not a bad thing, but *we will learn economy if we force ourselves to use absolutely only the language that we need to develop the compact plus core idea.* So on the evening before you have to preach the following morning's daily Mass, take a look at the readings. See if the readings suggest a "lead" and use it as the core thought. Put it at the beginning of the first sentence and try to evolve it into an expression in a compact idea. But remember, just a page! Here is a homily for the Fourth Week in Ordinary Time, Wednesday year II (2 Sam 24:2, 9–7; Mark 6:1–6.)

DAVID'S HEART

When St. Benedict wrote that the goal of the monk is to "run with heart expanding the ways of God's commands" he may have been thinking of King David [a core thought finding expression in compact idea].

Never was a heart [development of the core metaphor] turned more inside out than David's. Never was a heart more like a slingshot: elastic, capable of skipping a beat, of correcting itself, and of moving on to the rhythmic and often bitter, intrepid momentum of God's wisdom. Never have the words "I have been foolish, Lord" fallen so freely and humbly from any king's lips. Though pursued and hunted by Saul, David sang one of Hebrew poetry's greatest laments when Israel's first king was killed. After stealing Bathsheba and engineering the cowardly execution of her husband, Uriah, David repented, was punished, and picked himself up again. Though he fought justly and fiercely with Absalom, he would have offered his own life in exchange for his rebel son. David's heart broke many times, only to be reassembled. No wonder that tradition reckons David as the composer of the Psalter. Just like those remarkable texts, the king ran a gamut of difficult emotions, not all of them wondrously fair.

> With a heart like a rainbow, King David seems consigned, like all of us, to God's creative mystery, eclipsed in the human subject. We knew that from that fateful day when we first saw him tending his flock in the field: "Do not look on his appearance…for the Lord looks on the heart."

The principle "less is more" is often applied to liturgy. It is equally applicable to the homily.

✔ Do the Unexpected

Those who communicate have a basic desire: to reach the receiver. As the Heath brothers put the question:

> How do we get our audience to pay attention to our ideas, and how do we maintain their interest when we need time to get the idea across? We need to violate people's expectations. We need to be counterintuitive.…We can engage people's curiosity over a long period of time by systematically "opening gaps" in their knowledge—and then filling those gaps.[16]

The commercial television industry has been especially good at using the unexpected to grab people's attention. Marketing strategists realize that in order to get the average viewer away from the busy distractions of multitasking, the ad campaign must be built on the unexpected, the surprising.

For the last few years or so, Geico Insurance has cast several erudite, world-weary cavemen doing television interviews. Other ads feature the hyper-histrionic Little Richard doing a dramatic interpretation of a woman who hit a deer with her car but, thanks to Geico, got her claim in right away and was able to enjoy her Thanksgiving Day. Then there is the signature little green gecko, who appears like the animal world's answer to the urbane British actor Michael Caine. Animation and digital cinematography allow for imaginative, fairly inexpensive surprises even for the most mundane products. One of the most popular of the 2008 Superbowl commercials was the thirty-second spot for Bridgestone Tires in which a small squirrel hops in the road for an acorn, sees a car, and starts to scream hysterically. He is joined by any number of forest creatures, together with the woman in the passenger seat of the oncoming car. At the last second, the car swerves and misses the squirrel. Finally the voice-over tag line at the end: "For drivers who want to get the most out of their cars, it's Bridgestone or nothing." That surprise was all that we needed to get us to open up and have our gap filled.

Surprise acts as a kind of emergency override when we confront something unexpected and our guessing machines fail. Things come to a halt, ongoing activities are interrupted, our attention focuses involuntarily on the event that surprised us. Unexpected ideas are more likely to stick because surprise makes us pay attention and think. That extra attention and thinking sear unexpected events into our memories. Surprise gets our attention. Sometimes the attention is fleeting, but in other cases surprise can lead to enduring attention. Surprise can prompt us to hunt for underlying causes, to imagine other possibilities, to figure out how to avoid surprises in the future.[17]

Made to Stick carefully distinguishes between surprises and gimmicks. If the surprise remains in the service of the core message, the idea will be powerful and stick.

THE HOMILY AND THE "UNEXPECTED"

Much of what we have seen in homiletic method relies on the unexpected. Eugene Lowry's "upsetting the equilibrium," which generally speaking is a key feature in narrative paradigms, rests on the surprise and the subsequent tension that prevails in the congregation. Paul Scott Wilson's Page One could surprise many with its take on "Trouble in the Bible" and "Trouble in the World." Those who come to the liturgy for an irenic experience might find themselves overtaken by Fr. Robert Waznak's opening for a homily on the Third Sunday of Lent (Year C):

> There are some priests who should never be priests.
> There are some physicians who should never be
>   physicians.
> Many of these priests and physicians are certainly
>   smart enough to do their work.
> They fail not because of lack of smarts.
> They fail because of lack of hope.[18]

Waznak's surprise opens up a gap waiting to be filled. This opening is not gimmickry to get our attention, but, rather, is an initiation of creative tension, an introduction to a little mystery to which the congregation responds: "Really? What does he mean by that? I've never thought of it that way." This illustrates that the element of surprise does not have to be utterly shocking like a Hitchcock thriller, just unexpected.

In addition to the surprise that is present on one level or another in any good narrative, we must say that every homily should bring the hearer into the world of the unexpected. If the homily is simply reinforcing the status quo, then it has neither named grace nor named the demons in the community. That is not to say that every homily must be an earthshaking proclamation, but that *every proclamation should reposition our expectations.* Christ's Gospel brings peace, but it also promises justice. We might recall that when Jesus told his hearers in Nazareth that his words were fulfilled in their hearing, he equated that completion with liberty for captives, sight for the blind, freedom for the oppressed, and a year of favor from the Lord. These activities require a new hearing, a jarring of our expectations, so that we are convicted by the Word of God in our midst. Jesus as Word is the long-expected bringer of the unexpected. That is the double-edged sword. "I have come to bring fire to the earth," says Jesus. "And how I wish it were blazing already." The advent of his coming has opened up an unexpected gap that longs to be fulfilled in the Kingdom of God. That said, the preacher ought to remember the claim that the Word of God has on *him*, as we noted in Step One. That step calls anyone who preaches the Gospel to conversion and to an encounter with the God of love as revealed in Christ Jesus. The Incarnate Word has "decentered our expectations" by God's entry into human history. Preaching the Word of God mirrors the graced reality of Christ—God in the world.

✔ Be Concrete

Anyone who writes for a living knows the importance of using just the right word in order to convey an idea, an emotion, or a situation. The writer's intentions are embedded in the *particulars* of language, not in its abstractions. There is a huge difference between saying, "Mary looked nervous that evening," and saying, "After an unusually satisfying dinner of risotto and veal marsala, Mary lit a cigarette while her right hand trembled slightly, yet noticeably." *The more concrete our language, the closer we are to marrying the idea with the hearer.* "Naturally sticky ideas are full of concrete images—ice-filled bathtubs, apples with razors—because our brains are wired to remember concrete data....Speaking concretely is the only way to ensure that our idea will mean the same thing to everyone in our audience," say the Heath brothers.[19] They continue—

> Language is often abstract, but life is not abstract. Teachers teach students about battles and animals and books. Doctors repair problems with our stomachs, backs, and hearts. Companies create software, build planes, distribute newspapers; they build cars that are cheaper, faster, or fancier than last year's. Even the most abstract business strategy must eventually show up in the tangible actions of human beings. It's easier to understand those tangible actions than to understand an abstract strategy statement—just as it's easier

to understand a fox dissing some grapes than an abstract commentary about the human psyche.... Abstraction makes it harder to understand an idea and to remember it.[20]

The barrier to concrete language is "abstractspeak," which is a temptation that everyone in communication faces. Why? Ideas are usually abstract entities themselves and require a translation into the concrete. Preachers have to get the left side of their brains to communicate with the right side. Preachers must learn to speak in concrete terms, translating what *could* be into what *is*. Like good writers, *preachers must be attentive observers of the world in all its detail*. This is what Anne Lamott has to say about writing, which could easily be applied to preachers: "This is our goal as writers, I think; to help others have this sense of—please forgive me—wonder, of seeing things anew, things that can catch us off guard, that break in on our small, bordered worlds. When this happens, everything feels more spacious."[21] It is the job of the poet to take what is not tangible and make it real. What does God's joy look like? According to the Persian mystic poet Rumi, God's joy looks like this:

> God's joy moves from unmarked box to unmarked
>   box,
> From cell to cell. As rainwater, down into flowerbed.
> As roses, up from ground.
> Now it looks like a plate of rice and fish,
> Now a cliff covered with vines,
> Now a horse being saddled.
> It hides within these,
> Till one day it cracks them open.[22]

Beyond the obvious sensory experience that such description provides, there is an advantage to concrete language: concrete language gathers people of different strata together. "Concrete language helps people, especially novices, understand new concepts. Abstraction is the luxury of the expert. If you've got to teach an idea to a room full of people, and you aren't certain what they know, concreteness is the only safe language."[23] Description in detail gets everyone on the same page.

THE HOMILY AND THE "CONCRETE"

When Isaiah interprets his vocation to preach, he says, "The Lord God has given me / the tongue of a teacher, / that I may know how to sustain / the weary with a word. / Morning by morning he wakens— / wakens my ear / to listen as those who are taught" (50:4). Good teachers translate what appears to be incomprehensible material into concrete language for their students. Week after week, the faithful come to the Eucharistic Liturgy searching for meaning that only the Lord can provide. Are we going to answer those hungers of the human heart with abstractions? The Word of God is anything but abstract, and came to dwell among us as a human being. God did not become "humanness" but a man, Jesus, born at a particular place in time. He is "the image of the invisible God," Paul tells the Colossians (1:15). Consequently, images are the language of the preacher, the sinews that bring life to the Word of God.

Allowing the hearer to image the Word of God repositions the hearer, and that can only be done through an imaginative retelling through stories and images that change our lives. If we want to change the way people behave, we must alter the way they think. New thinking requires a repositioning through language. Jesus' parabolic preaching was intended to cause a profound shift—morally, intellectually, affectively—in his hearers. That language of the Kingdom is the business of the preacher, which is, more often than not, at odds with the language of the dominant culture. Redemptorist Jim Wallace describes how images in preaching work:

> Images surround and constantly clamor for our attention. Periodically one takes up root in our lives in a way that bears fruit again and again. This fruit can be

healthy or poisonous. The preacher can make a contribution to the faith life of the community by offering
images that seed the community's imagination. The
preacher will set before the community images from
the text that are sometimes set in tension with images
from the ongoing life of the community. Sometimes the
text challenges life, but life can also challenge the text.
Or images are offered that can be contemplated for
their own sake, either as characters that can live with
us, or a moment in a story that resonates and illumines
our experiences.[24]

Images well chosen function to gather the diverse community
and root the congregation in the concrete here and now of the
living God. Concrete language tells the baptized community that
God is present and alive, ready to act in the lives of all people.
To live in the concrete world of the imagination is to abide in
grace, to dwell in the Word made visible.

How concrete can we be? Very. To be honest, preachers can
never be too concrete. I would guess that few people genuinely
complain after a homily that the images were too vivid and that
they preferred abstract language instead. Try this exercise. Go
through the biblical text and pick a passage. What is it doing?
Figure out a way of saying it concretely. Ask: What does this
look like? Take, for instance, John's Gospel, chapter 17, the
beautiful prayer of Jesus to the Father. Verse 4: "I have glorified
you on earth by finishing the work that you gave me to do."
That little statement is intensely theological, magnificent; one
could write volumes that fill libraries on that single sentence.
Theologians over the ages have done so. But what does it *look*
like? What does it look like when Jesus glorified the Father by
finishing the work that he was given? How about this: "It looks
like a green vine, wet with dark purple grapes that are at their
peak, heavy in the hot sun and ready for harvest. It looks like
the moon at full bloom blinding even the night. It looks like a
ball of fire that has come from out of nowhere, radiant, sus-

pended, teasing us with its delicious heat." That is one way to test ourselves with making language less abstract, to take what appears not so concrete and put some sinews on it. There is a poet in every preacher!

✔ Be Credible

Credibility is all about relationship. "Sticky ideas have to carry their own credentials," says *Made to Stick*. We know anecdotally that successful ad campaigns—either in print or on television—thrive on trusting the spokesperson. That may mean glamorous stars doing hair-color commercials or the familiar face of Ed McMahon doing an endorsement for Publisher's Clearing House. What matters is the relationship underneath. Commenting on Sedelmaier's "Where's the Beef?" series of commercials featuring the eighty-year-old Clara Peller, who famously squints like an old curmudgeon and utters the line that would make her a celebrity, the Heath brothers say,

> There's a lot to love about these commercials. They're funny and well produced. Clara Peller became a minor celebrity. More remarkably, the ads highlighted a true advantage of Wendy's hamburgers. They really did have more beef. The ads were a refreshing departure from the standard advertiser tool kit that attempts to paint powerful but irrelevant emotions on consumer goods—for instance, associating a mother's love of her children with a particular brand of fabric softener. Wendy's did something more admirable: it highlighted a genuine advantage of its product and presented it in an enjoyable way.[25]

The Heath brothers' point here should not be taken lightly. Wendy's could have weighed in on statistics, proving that there was more beef in their burgers than in McDonald's or Burger King. Instead of drawing on "internal credibility," Wendy's discovered a new source of credibility—the audience. "Wendy's outsourced its credibility to its customers."[26] An eighty-year-old woman became the credible witness to allow the audience to see that there really was more beef to a Wendy's hamburger. These witnesses become "testable credentials," which far outweigh the statistics and data that ad campaigns might deploy in order to prove their product is far superior to others on the market.

THE HOMILY AND "CREDIBLE"

Christian preachers today face a credibility issue as never before. The congregation is living in a postmodern age in which Christopher Hitchens's *God Is Not Great*, Richard Dawkins's *The God Delusion*, and Sam Harris's *Letter to a Christian Nation* were on many bestseller lists. It is easy to be dismissive about such atheistic discourse—much of it misinformed and without theological merit—but the wise preacher would best attend to the sound of these growing voices in our culture that are antagonistic to any form of worship. The violent aspects of religion have been exposed over the last decade, especially with the tragic events of 9/11 and our violently aggressive intervention in Iraq and Afghanistan. Every day there is another suicide bomber, more often than not associated with a fanatical take on religion. Many nonreligious people rightly ask where God is in all this violence in the name of holiness. The congregation asks the same question. That is all the more reason why preachers face a credibility issue. That credibility became even more jeopardized after the news broke about the sex abuse scandal in the Catholic Church. And one more thing: the bad news has a lot of credibility—vivid pictures on the television don't lie.

I think that one way of approaching a congregation that faces a credibility issue is for the preacher to deal with a kind of hidden lie that may be hidden in the congregation. Tom Long says that there are hidden, essential lies that those who preach funerals should attend to, such as "doubts about the presence, power and goodness of God."[27] Long suggests that we are not the first to be plagued by God's absence: "Lord, if you had been here, our brother would not have died," says Martha to Jesus in

John 11:21. Similarly, outside the context of funerals, the Christian congregation is troubled and distracted by lies all week long—God's absence, the unreality of hope, the uselessness of faith, the impossibility of divine love—that the preacher must face-off, confront, and unmask as untruth. Here we cannot sufficiently emphasize the importance of preaching doctrine in such a way so that this teaching establishes the credibility of the tradition that has emerged out of the proclaimed Word. This credibility is literally a tactic of *credere*, the preaching of Christian eloquence that deepens faith and belief.

The answer to establishing credibility is not in facts or data alone. Preachers will always have facts available to them when preaching—on the scriptural text, catechetical teaching, liturgical practices—but how and when to deploy these facts becomes an issue of great importance. We can go on and on about the fact that John's Gospel says this and Mark does not, but these details do not make the Good News credible or not.

What does make the Gospel credible is a relationship that the Christian assembly develops with the preacher and the faith-experience he shares from the deep prayer resources of the text. For Aristotle, the *ethos* (or the speaker's interior world and personality), together with the *logos* and *pathos*, was a principal part of the "speech act." It would be hard to exaggerate the importance of the preacher as a credible witness. "The homilist is an indispensable figure in ensuring that today's Catholics do not become strangers to 'the faith of the church.' To help his people know and live the riches of the faith of the church, which is 'their' faith, the homilist needs to think and preach doctrinally.'"[28]

At the same time, there is inestimable value of potential Christian witness in the pulpit. There are preachers who have very little skills at oratory, but remain highly credible because of their ability to witness. The priest who baptized me as an infant, Fr. Murphy, was notoriously soft-spoken, but people strained to hear him precisely because of the value of his *ethos*, which transmitted his credible Christian witness. We know from studies in communication that as much as 80 to 90 percent of actualizing a message relies on nonverbal signals. People *want* to identify with the speaker; the authenticity of the messenger is crucial to creating a relationship of credibility. It is as if the very foundations of credibility echo from the preacher who is a true witness to the Gospel: *credo*; he brings with him Scripture and Tradition, and that from his lifetime, a life spent in prayer and service, all collapsed into a ten-minute homily. Once that credible relationship has been established between the preacher and the congregation, the message of the Gospel will stick. A vital question for any preacher to ask at the time of prayer is: "How credible am I to the people I serve?" That is a soul-searching question that obviously involves much more than rhetorical skills. Credibility is bound up with trust, relationship, and faith; any pastor knows how key these values are to building a parish community. Credibility is the pastoral link for preaching and so much else in ministry. Without credibility, the homily may be amusing, but the Christian community will eventually ask the question: "Where is God in all this?"

✔ Use Emotions

If you have ever wondered, as I have, why Madison Avenue pays so much attention to casting decisions, we need look no further than "emotions." People relate to characters and will invest in them emotionally—and financially, from the commercial perspective!

> Research shows that people are more likely to make a charitable gift to a single needy individual than to an entire impoverished region. We are wired to feel things for people, not for abstractions. For instance, it's difficult to get teenagers to quit smoking by instilling in them a fear of the consequences, but it's easier to get them to quit by tapping into their resentment of the duplicity of Big Tobacco.[29]

Dan and Chip Heath cite no less a personage than Blessed Mother Teresa of Calcutta to back up their claim that people are persuaded by an individual connection to a person rather than an appeal to statistics or an abstraction. "If I look at the mass, I will never act. If I look at the one, I will."[30] Survey after survey indicates the same thing: Getting people to care and having them take action depend on an emotional connection. Drawing on the research of Abraham Maslow, the Heath brothers say that advertisers have to use associations, appeal to self-interest, and appeal to identity. Typically, nonprofit organizations want to get people to look beyond their own self-interests. But this seems to appeal to an analytic side of the human subject, which is less effective than a pitch toward associations, and, ironically, self-interest and identity. *Made to Stick* reminded me of a commercial that appeared some decades ago when we were just starting to think about the ethical issues involved with saving the planet. An antilitter campaign began using a Native American, who walked through a plastic-riddled forest. Cut to a close-up, and there was a tear coming down the cheek of the grief-stricken man. The problem here in this commercial is that the folks who litter would not associate themselves with Native Americans in the first place. When Texas started its own antilitter series, it used the slogan "Don't Mess with Texas," using Dallas Cowboys defensive end Ed "Too-Tall" Jones and defensive tackle Randy White picking up trash on the highway.[31] Associations with the right group get the viewer to aspire to be like the performer—in this case, perform an altruistic act.

Emotions function as avenues to motivation.

How can we get people to care about our ideas? We get them to take off their Analytical Hats. We create empathy for specific individuals. We show how our ideas are associated with things that people already care about. We appeal to their self-interest, but we also appeal to their identities—not only to the people they are right now but also to the people they would like to be.[32]

THE HOMILY AND "EMOTIONS"

Fulfilled in Your Hearing emphasizes the "personal" quality of the homily. That does not mean that the preacher should be chatty, but instead should *aim for transparency in preaching.* Few things are worse than an arrogant preacher who positions himself as better than the congregation, either directly (illustrations of his virtue) or indirectly (aloofness, distant tone). The congregation should sense that the preacher is speaking to them from inside their own space; a pastoral connection in preaching is an emotional one. The homilist becomes associated with their group faith-experience, a conduit into the Gospel. Moreover, the process of induction itself invites an exploration into emotions because such a narrative process is experiential and avoids abstractions. The very tools that the congregation will draw on will be, at least in part, affective. More important, the question of emotions and its use in the homily answers the question "So what?" This is a motivational issue similar to the one faced by nonprofits during an ad campaign. The congregation may understand everything the preacher has said analytically, but does this cause the baptized Christian to act and behave differently? If there is an emotional connection, it will do so.

So the preacher must locate the contours of the focus of the homily in characters we care about. If the preacher gives an example of a person, we should know his or her name. What did that person look like? How old? Sometimes it is just a matter of an image or brief reference, but these illustrations should have a human face. Also, as we have seen from the *Spiritual Exercises* of St. Ignatius Loyola and from other sources, the characters in the Bible should be expanded and filled out during the preacher's private meditation and *lectio divina.* They are not abstract principles on two feet, but flesh and blood. They should live emotionally in the prayer life of the preacher. The most important person in this regard is Jesus Christ himself. Do you have a conversation with the Lord in prayer while praying over a particular pericope? What do you want to ask him? In the end, the preacher is always being *re*-converted every time he prays into a biblical passage that he is preparing to preach. What does the crowd look like that sat around Jesus when he preached the Beatitudes? Fleshing out one or two individuals may be a marvelous point of departure for a homily free from abstraction. If preachers are inviting the congregation to take off their "analytical hats," then he needs to provide a landscape that is lush with characters with whom his assembly can associate themselves.

These characters become vehicles for self-transcendence because they appeal to the sensibility of those who would like to be like that one day. Imagine giving a homily for teenagers that focused on self-giving, while filling out the character of the young man who brought the disciples five loaves and two fish! That is not an abstraction about altruism, but an invitation to become one who feeds the multitudes. Finally, contemporary illustrations that involve the character of individuals and their specific human struggles and successes are great. These examples put skin on ideals, concepts, and principles; they are emotional vehicles that grant access to the deeper world of the congregation, one that comes alive when faced with a homily that breathes life.

✔ Tell Stories

Now that we have reached the last of the Heath brothers' acronym SUCCESs, it should be clear that each of these suggestions is largely interrelated and that they support one another. The appeal to emotions that angles toward an association with a particular character will thrive, for instance, if there is concrete language and credible evidence to witness. The paradigm as a whole asks us to move away from abstractions. That insistence is especially true for their last category, stories. Emotions will always be more engaged when stories are involved.

> How do we get people to act on our ideas? We tell stories. Firefighters naturally swap stories after every fire, and by doing so they multiply their experience; after years of hearing stories, they have a richer, more com-

plete mental catalog of critical situations they might confront during a fire and the appropriate responses to those situations. Research shows that mentally rehearsing a situation helps us perform better when we encounter that situation in the physical environment. Similarly, hearing stories acts as a kind of mental flight simulator, preparing us to respond more quickly and effectively.[33]

Linking a diet with a personal story has proved very successful. A few hours north of St. Meinrad School of Theology, a young man in Bloomington, Indiana, was diagnosed by his roommate with edema, a chronic condition that made Jared Folgel weigh 425 pounds and gain a sixty-inch waist. He started eating SUBWAY sandwiches for both lunch and dinner and walking more. A 1999 article in the Indiana University's school newspaper, the *Indiana Daily Student*, contained a quotation that any merchandiser would kill for: "SUBWAY® helped save my life and start over. I can't ever repay that."[34] That statement became the basis of a very successful campaign. Note that all the elements of the Heath brothers' SUCCESs formula are here: Simple—eat SUBWAY and lose weight; Unexpected—weight lost using fast food; Concrete—oversized pants, diet of particular sandwiches; Credible—an actual college student, before-and-after pictures; Emotional—a common concern, feelings of desperation, a regular person we can identify with; Story—the personal story of Jared Folgel, whom we care about more than stats, and who reached his potential through SUBWAY. The story allows us to see that "our protagonist overcomes big odds to triumph. It inspires the rest of us to do the same."[35]

The story of Jared, according to the Heath brothers, is a classic *Challenge plot*, something like David and Goliath. "There are variations of the Challenge plot that we all recognize: the underdog story, the rags-to-riches story, the triumph of sheer willpower over adversity."[36] Perhaps one of the things that make the story so palatable is that Americans tend to root for the underdog. When the story can engage folks on such a deep level and allow them to participate in their own triumph ("I can do this too!"), then the story has indeed been an effective one. I would go so far as to suggest that we learned much of the shape of this kind of story from our own religious tradition, where God has defeated and overcome the power of sin and death through victory in Christ. The Old Testament is bursting with God's love for the marginalized, the defeated, the disinherited. How many times have we seen Jesus champion the underdog in the Gospel, from lepers to the woman caught in adultery? And the Christian community participates in the struggle of sinners in the Bible who have been healed by God's loving hand. Those who see their own autobiography in the contours of such biblical characters say, "God can do great things for me as well!"

The Heath brothers suggest two other plots that have been just as effective in narrative culture. The *Connection plot's* paradigm does, in fact, have its blueprint in the Bible with the story of the Good Samaritan. This story is all about crossing the great cultural divide between Samaritan and Jew. But in modern terms, this crossover can be any movement from one faction or group to a separate other. I'd imagine that the plethora of ads for medicines have some roots in the Good Samaritan Connection plot. Mother comes to the rescue with just the right cough medicine in the middle of the night, crossing the boundaries of sickness and health, night and light, for the child in distress. Lastly, the *Creativity plot* involves someone "making a mental breakthrough, solving a long-standing puzzle, or attacking a problem in an innovative way. It's a MacGyver plot."[37] I think that this Creativity plot could be another version of the underdog with a great idea—something like a Challenge plot.

THE HOMILY AND "STORY"

I have been detailing the use of narrative throughout the last few steps on the Ladder of Preaching, but narrative preaching may or may not include story. At the same time, the homily and the story are natural allies. Edmund Steimle, Charles Rice, and

Morris Niedenthal's *Preaching the Story* (1980) helped to revolutionize the way we think of homilies as conveyers of meaning through images, symbols, and, indeed, the lives of others. The Bible is itself a collection of stories of faith revealed in the context of graced religious experience. It is a mixture of all three of the plots that *Made to Stick* describes. The preacher needs to recognize the parallels that might exist between these biblical plots and more contemporary ones that help to transform them into a modern parable. Surely there are such Challenge plots in and out of the parish that could be gleaned for story illustrations in homilies. If we are preaching on the story of the Good Samaritan, we might discover a contemporary "Connection plot" that illustrates Jesus' famous parable. Finding a parallel plot allows the congregation to own the biblical parable in a new way. When they hear that an African American woman from Chicago's South Side donated one of her kidneys to a white teenager living in Lincoln Park, it strikes a cord (Connection plot); we are no longer living in first-century Palestine but the United States with its racial divides. It is transposing plots like this that allows Jesus' original message to break through to the twenty-first century.

A well-placed story can make all the difference in a homily. When things seem to be going abstract for the hearer, it is time to rethink that portion of the homily again and think in story. Narratives have been the great motivating principle in Western culture. The story of salvation and the life of Jesus are the foundation of Christian living. What better place for a story than a homily?

MISSTEPS

✗ *The faulty assumption that secular culture—particularly commercial enterprise—has nothing much to offer the religious community.*

That backward-thinking claim, as we have suggested earlier, has been refuted by the Church itself on a number of occasions. There are specious ecclesial issues embedded in this argument, most notably those which refuse to be in dialogue with contemporary culture.

✕ *The use of ordination or ecclesial status, rather than the Word of God, to function exclusively as the authority of the message.*

I emphasize the word *exclusively* because, clearly, there should be a level of credibility granted by ordination that imbues the preacher with a genuine aura of credibility. I take that as a given, to be sure. But if the preacher relies entirely on his status as an ecclesial minister, he will always be less effective than if he trusts in the power of the Word of God to transform the lives of others. The Spirit helps us in our weakness to cry "Abba, Father," and so we have the courage to proclaim, using words we have heard from the depths of out hearts. Genuine witness must come from within. To paraphrase Aristotle, when orators use their rank to persuade an audience, the crowd may be swayed by the ethos of the prestige, but such oratory is not artistic. The preacher needs to rely on contemporary rhetorical strategies whatever his ecclesial position might be.

✕ *The tendency to be abstract.*

Much of what the Heath brothers suggest in *Made to Stick* is a guard against abstraction, but theological speculation often pulls against the attempts for concreteness and story-filled homilies. Many of the missteps in this area of abstract thinking could be avoided if the preacher asked himself a simple question: "What are the *listeners* making of my language?" If there is vagueness or mushy language that is abstract, ask a second question: "What does what I am saying really *look* like?" And finally, "What are listeners *feeling* as a result of my words?" This strategy applies to doctrinal illustrations as well as scriptural ones. St. Thomas Aquinas explained the most abstract of theological concepts by analogy. Some of the greatest theologians were also great pastors because they were able to teach doctrine in ways that allowed the faithful to deepen their faith *concretely*.

X *The temptation to deploy a story—with its concrete, emotional detail intact—but one that either overwhelms the Gospel or has very little to do with the readings.*

Resist this tendency. Images and stories should be chosen judiciously. There is nothing like a parallel between the Bible and a contemporary story for bringing home an insight, but there is no point in telling a story if the tale has very little to do with the focus statement. With regard to stories, preachers return to the focus statement as a company would return to a mission statement: that mandate gives us the license to act.

QUESTIONS AND PROJECTS FOR CLASS

1. Ask students to bring a print ad to class. What is the guiding question in the ad? In other words, what is the rhetoric of this particular advertisement asking me to do? Can the class name several tactics in the ad?

2. Assign a one-page paper, asking the class to analyze how a recent film or TV ad plays to a particular audience.

3. Assign students to write a one-page homily, using one of the following tactics: simple, unexpected, concrete, credible, emotional, stories.

QUESTIONS FOR REFLECTION

1. Are you conscious of contemporary methods of persuasion, particularly in the media? If not, be attentive

to advertisements and try to develop an eye and ear for the rhetoric of technology.

2. How do stories affect you? Do you identify with certain characters? Which stories in the Bible move you?

3. Who is the most credible person in our society? Why?

Step Six

GLOBALIZING THE HOMILY FOR A NEW EVANGELIZATION

Vayan, pues, y hagan que todos los pueblos sean mis discípulos.

—Matthew 28:19

The Cathedral of St. Bavo in Ghent houses one of the greatest masterpieces in the history of Western art. Completed in 1430–1432 by the Van Eyck brothers, the Ghent Altarpiece comprises twenty-four panels of key figures and moments in salvation history. The most famous of these panels shares the title of the entire work: *The Adoration of the Lamb of God.* This is an astonishing, stunning representation of the Eucharistic Liturgy at the end-time, celebrated around the Lamb of God, Christ Jesus, whose blood pours out from his wounded side into a gold chalice on an altar richly embroidered in red brocade. Set on an idyllic green landscape of lush trees and river valleys, the altar and the Lamb are surrounded by angels, Old Testament kings and prophets, New Testament apostles and disciples, confessors and virgins. Even in the midst of such a gathering, it is striking how each figure stands out as a distinct individual. Far from being a collection of typical faces and bodily postures, Flemish masters like the Van Eyck brothers famously painted every exquisite human detail. Indeed, the panel is ultimately a collection of individual lives captured at a breathtaking, apocalyptic moment. At the base of the altar there is a fountain of running water, where there is inscribed that this source is the water of life that springs from the throne of the Lamb. The Lamb himself looks directly at the spectator as if to draw us in at this moment of great intimacy into his magisterial and salvific presence.

The Adoration of the Lamb of God is a vision of the New Jerusalem and our own. It is an invitation to respond to the proclamation of the angel who directed the Evangelist John, on the island of Patmos, to say, "Write this: Blessed are those who are invited to the marriage supper of the Lamb" (Rev 19:9). Could we imagine anything more blessed than the diversity of humanity called to worship before Christ Jesus to give praise and thanksgiving? It is both our privilege and our challenge to live in the twenty-first century, an unprecedented period of multi-cultural diversity. With a rich tapestry of African American, Hispanic, and Asian cultures woven into parishes like never before, it is the language of the Lamb that will draw them together. Simple gifts: bread made body and wine made blood, done in remembrance of him who died for us.

The Lamb invites all people and nations into the Feast of his Body and Blood. And yet before these diverse groups gather at the table of the Eucharist, they come to hear at the table of the Word. That the Church is multicultural may be nothing new, but its witness to peace, justice, and universal fellowship could not be timelier in a world of postmodern fragmentation. Indeed, globalization, when read through the lens of Christian witness, remains an eschatological sign of God's future, the Kingdom promised us by Christ when all are made one in the blood of the Lamb.

The preacher's challenge in Step Six, then, builds on the previous steps by drawing from a rich interior life that has responded to the Word of God in the midst of a knowing, contemporary homiletic strategy that is aware of the hearers. But this step also asks some important questions about the preacher's relationship with the hearers and himself: If there is so vast a multitude to be preached to, what kind of conversion must the ordained minister of the Gospel undergo in order to make the proclamation of Jesus authentic, timely, and pastoral? Confronting the multicultural aspect of preaching takes the ordained minister into the deepest corners of himself to conversion, a quality that Mark O'Keefe has identified as one of the three evocative aspects of the priestly calling.[1] With the globalization of the Church at the horizon of just about every ambo of every denomination in the United States, how can the homilist gather a diverse group into the communion of the Word of God, while recognizing that he too must stand before the Lamb, mindful of his calling to preach the Gospel to all nations?

A POINT OF DEPARTURE: DISMANTLING OUR SECURITIES

For reasons of space and practicality, I will cover the fascinating and broad topic of multicultural preaching in a space smaller than this area deserves. Multicultural preaching, as I have suggested more fully elsewhere,[2] clearly finds it origins in the word *culture* itself. And we can begin to understand multiculturalism only when we realize that, in the words of African American homiletics professor Henry Mitchell, "Culture is the accumulation over time of all the wisdom and methods of a given cultural group, for the purpose of ensuring its survival."[3] But first, a clarification: When I speak of "multicultural preaching," I am not referring here to those who are called to preach and celebrate the liturgy in a more or less specialized language group; those who find themselves in a particular ministry devoted to what Kenneth G. Davis and others refer to as "cross-cultural preaching." So in the area of Hispanic preaching one would find wise advice in Justo L. González and Pablo A. Jiménez's *Púlpito* (Nashville: Abingdon Press, 2005). Or those involved in the Korean community might find Jung Young Lee's *Korean Preaching* helpful (Nashville: Abingdon Press, 1997). There are multiple resources available to the preacher in the African American community as well, such as those by Henry Mitchell and Frank Thomas.[4] I am adjudicating between these terms not to prefer one over the other, so much as to limit my focus here because of space. Where appropriate, however, I will make references to both of these important aspects of preaching in the context of the multicultural landscape.

Preaching to a diverse, multicultural congregation involves a somewhat different strategy from those I have just mentioned, particularly because of the need to access the varied experience and accumulated wisdom of the assembly, one that may be shared with the preacher in the most minimal of ways. A reference to the Ladder of Preaching will be appropriate here, since the first five steps involve a process of conversion and reconstruction, beginning with a foundational relationship with the Word. By Step Six and Step Seven, this movement upward continues its intensity, particularly around self-confrontation. Preaching will always demand of us a conversion on many different levels. Globalizing the homily asks us to put aside our preconceptions of our role as preachers and honor the assembly as Christ himself. After a number of years, it is only natural for preachers to settle into a preconceived role of preaching. And yet, multicultural preaching requires that we rethink our relationship with the congregation as never before. Effective multicultural preaching presupposes a moral conversion in which the living Body of Christ, in unity, is represented by the diversity of the human family. Simply being aware of our prejudices is an initial foray into preaching to those who are different from me.

In a marvelous lecture on homiletics in the context of diversity, Archbishop Wilton Gregory's 2008 lecture, "Preaching in the Multicultural Context of the U.S.," raised several points of what he termed *"misconceptions" in speaking of the Latino, African American, and Asian communities*. One of the most formidable, I think, is a willingness to live in the complexity of the multicultural event by rethinking our role as preacher. Here is one misconception: *"In the preaching event, roles are clearly and irrevocably defined: We are the preachers or teachers, and they are learners."*[5] This is the call for conversion in preaching. In a certain sense, the entire Ladder of Preaching has been designed precisely to help preachers rethink, redefine, and reestablish their roles; however, *metanoia* for effective homiletics is especially crucial for preaching multiculturally:

> When we walk into a new community, one that is not our own, we may hesitate and have our own self-doubts even at an unconscious level. One remedy, again not even consciously embraced, is to assert within ourselves a clarity of our role in the face of the unclear situation we are about to encounter....In this lack of clarity, there is always the temptation to seize some clarity at all costs, even it if is not true clarity. I can, for example, narrowly understand the roles we play in the preaching encounter. I preach and teach, and they listen and learn. In crossing over to preach in cultural contexts other than our own, the roles are not so clearly and irrevocably defined....Especially in the cross-cultural context, the preacher must also listen and learn. Despite our own propensity to claim a clear role in the preaching process, there is more to the story than we would expect.[6]

Archbishop Gregory's comments are appropriate whether we are preaching to a single ethnic group or multiple cultures gathered at the same altar. Gregory's claim here is contemporary and missiological; the preacher must rethink his comfortable relationship with the priestly roles that have helped to define his ministry. Archbishop Gregory draws from his own experience with working with the Vietnamese community when he says that "there is so much I cannot know or fully understand as I stand before these faithful Catholic people whose faith has been proven in so many ways."[7] If we are able to admit that "there is so much [we] cannot know or fully understand" about the people we serve, then we are really ready to listen to the hearer— the multicultural hearer. *It is at this point that the Ladder of*

Preaching meets St. Benedict's Ladder of Humility. In order to reach the heights of evangelism for the sake of the Gospel of Christ, I must descend into the path of humility and self-forgetfulness.

Practically speaking, the question we might ask ourselves to help guide our discussion is this: What are the preaching models that I have absorbed and in which have I been most comfortable over the years? The late Robert Waznak has proposed four models of preaching, which are a kind of checklist for those engaging in homiletics. Actually, these models could be reviewed at any time in the course of a journey up the Ladder of Preaching, but based on Archbishop Gregory's insightful observations about the shifting roles of preaching, these make a useful inventory when discussing multicultural communication. Waznak offers his observations about the advantages and disadvantages of all these models, but for our purposes here, I will read them through the lens of multicultural preaching.

Herald

The herald is a key model in preaching because it is linked to the most frequently used word in the New Testament, *kērussein* ("to proclaim"). This kind of preaching focused on the Good News that Jesus died and rose again. Jesus' injunction to Mary Magdalene to tell the disciples what she had seen is an invitation to herald the Gospel. Although the herald finds its antecedents in apostolic preaching, the heraldic or *kerygmatic* preacher did not become strong in Catholic circles, according to Waznak, until the Austrian theologian Josef Jungmann, SJ, "emphasized the proclamation of the Good News. Kerygmatic preaching and teaching focused on the kerygma or the core of the gospel preached by the apostles: the saving acts of God in Christ. Jungmann deplored the preaching of his day which he said was no more than a 'vulgarization of theological tracts.'"[8]

The *advantages* of preaching as herald are clear enough. The core message from the revealed Word of God is universal and foundational. The herald responds to Jesus' admonition to preach to all nations and does so out of a distinctive charism. In a diverse assembly, the core message of the Good News gathers people of different backgrounds "into the one Body of Christ a living sacrifice of praise." Prophetically, Vatican II urged kerygmatic preaching in a time when the world was becoming a global network and needed the proclamation of the Good News to distant lands. The *disadvantage* of preaching as herald multiculturally is potentially ignoring the *context* of preaching—a vital component to understanding the local and diverse community. This factor is especially urgent in the Latino, Korean, and other immigrant communities that face the threat of deportation because of the discriminatory immigration laws in this country. Therefore, in his apostolic exhortation "On Evangelization in the Modern World," Pope Paul VI says, "This is why evangelization involves an explicit message adapted to the different situations constantly being realized, about the rights and duties of every human being, about family life...about international life, peace, justice and liberation—a message especially energetic about liberation."[9] Preachers might lose the zeal for being an exegete for the Christian assembly and the distinctiveness of the hearer if they lean too heavily into the model of the herald.

Witness

In "On Evangelization in the Modern World," Paul VI says further that people in the present age are looking for "authenticity" and "truth and honesty." Indeed, "Modern man listens more willingly to witnesses than to teachers, and if he does listen to teachers, it is because they are witnesses....The world is calling for evangelizers to speak to it of a God whom the evangelists themselves should know and be familiar with as if they could see the invisible."[10] The document anticipated the universal language of witness as an instrument for spreading the Gospel. Pope Paul VI was underlining the "witness value" that all baptized Christians are called to live. In this regard, preachers actualize witness value in an important and vital way, especially in multicultural settings where the experience of the one who proclaims the Gospel grants an authenticity to the message. If there is a language barrier, then personal witness transcends linguistic meaning. As Anna Carter Florence has demonstrated, "preaching as testimony" has carried a lot of authority in the history of the Christian church.[11] Undoubtedly, such witness value would add a lot of cachet to a preacher amid foreign-born, non-native speakers. Moreover, the transparency that preaching as witness requires lends itself to reaching out to those who are themselves on the margins of society.

Witness value also articulates justice. Where would we be without the witness preaching of the civil rights movement, where Dr. King lived a Gospel vision that brought him "to the mountain top" so that his eyes could see "the glory of the Lord"? On the other hand, witness preaching can be insulating and culturally insensitive to some ethnic groups. Does *my story as witness* really have much to say to a single Latina who has to take three jobs to support her extended family? For Waznak, "an ideal homily is a weaving of three stories: the stories of the preacher, of God, and of the listener."[12] But in many well-known instances in contemporary Christian preaching, the preacher's story eclipses God's and the listener's so that all that remains are a series of well-meaning, personal recollections by a self-styled raconteur. Witness preaching is harder than it appears, and engaging God's story as well as the listener's in a multicultural setting is still more challenging.

Teacher

The preacher as teacher has a long and venerable history in the Church. When St. Gregory the Great wrote his *Book on Pastoral Rule* with instructions for preachers, he framed that vocation from the perspective of a teacher. "Since, then, we have shown what manner of man the pastor ought to be, let us now set forth after what manner he should teach. For, as long before us Gregory Nazianzen of reverend memory has taught, one and the same exhortation does not suit all, inasmuch as neither are all bound together by similarity of character." So saying, Gregory then lays out a diverse prospectus for the preacher as teacher. For example, the preacher addresses "the kindly disposed and the envious. The simple and the insincere....Those that are at variance, and those that are at peace. Lovers of strife, and peacemakers."[13] Gregory's advice schools the wise pastoral teacher in the variety of congregants and enables the preacher to plan his discourse accordingly.

Yet, however helpful such tactics might be, the disadvantage is that the role of the teacher is reinscribed over and over again: The assembly is a group to be figured out; to be analyzed as an object and a vague mass of persons, however diverse; *to be preached into or preached at.* They are far from listening partners, emerging from a variety of cultures with different backgrounds. Clinging to the role of the teacher, as Archbishop Gregory suggests, tends to set up a wall between the assembly and the preacher, the other and myself. For pastoral reasons, we need to be able to let go of the role of teacher, at least for a time, and enter into a conversation with cultures different from my own. The congregation always has a lot to teach the preacher.

Parenthetically, I must say that I would like to qualify the role of teacher as preacher. I think that it is possible to distinguish between "teacher" and "teaching." Homiletics should be informed by sound doctrinal theology and teaching, as I have suggested throughout the Ladder of Preaching. But that does not mean that the preacher himself must *cling* to the role of the preacher as teacher. The Church, with its rich history and tradition, is the teacher, the *magister*; the preacher facilitates that teaching in the manner most appropriate to the local cultural setting. Indeed, more important, *the doctrine of the Church is a unifying presence in the midst of the diverse assembly, and its very language, spoken during the homily, knits together in catholicity those who may be diverse in so many other ways.* As I mentioned in a previous step and hope to demonstrate a bit later with a homily illustration, a doctrinal teaching can arise out of the biblical witness and allow the Word of God to instruct the baptized assembly. After all, the scriptures were the source of the Church's teachings in the first place. That process requires bringing some teaching into what the bishops' *Fulfilled in Your Hearing* refers to as "a mediator of meaning."

Interpreter

Although *Fulfilled in Your Hearing* tends to favor the preacher as interpreter, the document does so in order that the congregation might observe the contours of their own graced existence and give thanks and praise to the living God in the preaching act.

> The function of the Eucharistic homily is to enable people to lift up their hearts, to praise and thank the Lord for his presence in their lives. It will do this more effectively if the language it uses is specific, graphic, and imaginative. The more we can turn to the picture language of the poet and the storyteller, the more we will be able to preach in a way that invites people to respond from the heart as well as from the mind.[14]

As we have seen in previous examples and recommendations by professional communicators, there is an undeniable advantage to concrete language and images, especially in the contemporary scene. Evolving a visual grammar in the homily with a multicultural population helps to transcend difficult, abstract meanings. Moreover, the use of these images forms a kind of common denominator for the liturgical assembly, gathering a diverse people into the immediacy of the homiletic space. A formation takes place on the level of language because *the Christian assembly is making meaning in the very act of liturgical preaching itself, mediated by the preacher as interpreter*. Like Moses, the preacher as mediator stands in the breach between God and the people, speaking to the people as one who negotiates biblical, theological, and cultural understanding. More important, by hearing the Word of God effectively interpreted, the congregation names grace for itself inside a diverse assembly, each individual blessed by his or her own culture. David Buttrick refers to this interpretive skill as the primary task for the minister. "The primary task of ministry is not caring, for all kinds of people can offer devoted care; nor is it counseling, for there are able professionals who counsel; nor is it church management, for managers abound. No, the primary task of ministry is meaning."[15] Think of how crucial the role of the preacher as mediator of meaning would be for immigrants. The preacher as interpreter would help Latinos and Asians understand American culture through the lens of biblical narrative. Conversely, the homily might attend to helping the Anglo community hear the scriptures with Hispanic or Asian ears. Consider how the mediator of meaning might lend a word of freedom to many African American males who experience the social sin of racism in our country day after day. The interpreter returns always to Jesus, bringer of the freedom that only he can give in a world imprisoned by sin.

The difficulty with the preacher as interpreter and why it is perhaps the most difficult of all four models to follow is that the mediator of meaning will always be treading on new ground, especially in a multicultural assembly. Jesus went to Nazareth where he was savagely rejected (Luke 4:28–30). But then again, after Nazareth, Jesus preached in Capernaum, where he prophetically interpreted the Isaiah text (8:22—9:2) as an announcement of his own prophetic coming (in Matt 4:12–17) and spoke "with authority" (Luke 4:32). Two communities hearing the Word himself interpreted *by* himself, yet both reacting very differently to the intrepid proclamation. As we know, Jesus spent his entire ministry interpreting God through the unique and definitive relationship of his Sonship with the Father, even as he faced denunciation, humiliation, and death. To be a preacher who interprets the Word means letting go of roles altogether and allowing diverse others to speak and interpret as if they were, together, unwrapping a parable. Paradoxically, many come to the liturgy expecting to find clearly defined roles, wanting to see a black-

and-white distinction between the preacher and the congregation. Maybe that was the problem in Nazareth after all, a rigid
expectation of roles: "Is this not Joseph's son?" Good questions
for us, then, are: Can the preacher resist these temptations to
hold onto fixed roles? Can the congregation let these preconceived roles go in order to experience the Gospel in a radically
new way? Finally, the diverse congregation needs to be cate-
chized. Can the interpreter of meaning also negotiate the doctrine of the Church as a teaching, without injecting his own ego?

A sure way to integrate doctrine is to allow this teaching to
emerge out of the scriptures and not out of the authority of the
preacher alone. As I have suggested earlier, doctrinal and theological meaning are essential tools in the homiletic act. As Cardinal
Levada has reminded the Church,

> We tend to think of doctrine as something added to
> Scripture, but in fact doctrines are the result of a clus-
> ter of scriptural texts understood in a particular way.
> This is an understanding developed in the context of
> the church's faith, so that when the word of God is
> proclaimed in the liturgy, the *sensus fidei* of the faith-
> ful continues to be formed. When the homilist knows
> the clusters of texts that surround certain doctrines,
> then the appearance of these texts in a particular
> liturgy becomes an occasion for doctrinal teaching that
> is nonetheless thoroughly scriptural.[16]

As I have suggested, this relationship between the biblical
and the doctrinal can be a distinct advantage in multicultural
preaching because doctrine provides the preacher with a common ground with which to gather the diverse assembly. Indeed,
after the homily, the multicultural congregation will gather in
faith in the language of the Creed. These are common, shared
beliefs, symbols, truths, and historical realities. *If the assembly
has already witnessed the biblical world in close alliance with
doctrinal teaching, then this diverse assembly is ready to profess*

its faith together in unity and peace. The Word has gathered them—all peoples and nations, of every race and way of life—and waits to be born in the hearts of those who believe.

An example will illustrate this point. In certain ways, Jesus' encounter with the Samaritan woman at the well in John 4:5–42 is paradigmatic of the multicultural event: It is a foundational meeting of the outsider with the Christ who draws all people to the fount of living water. In the process of helping the woman recognize her own hunger, he also catechizes her with a new teaching—himself. The following homily from the Third Sunday of Lent, Year A (Exod 17:3–7; Ps 95:1–2, 6–7, 8–9; Rom 5:1–2, 5–8; John 4:5–42) is an excellent way to show how we might think about the biblical readings as being served by doctrine, particularly the teaching on baptism. Indeed, as many have observed, we ought not to discount the resources in the *Catechism of the Catholic Church* or homilies written by other authors, ancient and new, on important Church teaching; taken together, these represent an enormous fountain enabling the language of the homily to unify the congregation in concert with the scriptures for the day. Here, the Church's teaching on baptism clearly flows out of the readings for the Sunday.

WHERE LIFE BEGINS

Most of us know that we are governed by our needs from our first moments on earth. As anyone who has spent much time around children realizes, babies learn to cry, to yell, or to grasp from their early days in the crib. Some months after my nephew was born, I put my finger in his tiny fist and I thought: "This kid has got some grip." And yet grabbing and wanting is what children do in order to tell us what they need. In later years, most adults get beyond the needy stage, but we are still tempted to grasp for the shiny allurement dangling before our eyes. What is placed before us might be jingly new car keys, or another high-tech computer, or a larger house. And honestly, in the everyday world of commerce, we are encouraged along the way by ads that tell us: "Just do it." Or, "Obey your thirst."

The fact is that most of us live out of our wants and desires. That phenomenon is part of human nature. We can see the behavior coursing through history. Most of the heartbreak of humanity has emerged from an endless quest for power. That grasping for what we want might be seizing thrones of kings or emperors in the age of the Visigoths or the Medici, or overtaking governments and nations in the era of global politics and industrialization. We want what we want, in much the same way that ancient Israel demanded what they craved in the desert: water. It is not hard to understand the need for water in a dry, dusty land. But there is more to this account of Massah and Meribah in the Book of Exodus than a simple quest for water. Israel was brought out of Egypt, from the place of slavery, and still they distrusted both Moses and God. This young nation manages to forget all the miracles that God did to deliver them from a life of servitude. They are the chosen people at the edge of the Promised Land, and all they can seemingly muster up for a question is: "Why did you ever make us leave Egypt?" "We are thirsty!" We can see them, perhaps grasping not only for water from the rock, but also for the place they left behind. Blind to God's presence, Israel appears very ready to trade mature human freedom for the childish fulfillment of appetites in Egypt. It is very easy to forget that *we* too live out of our desires. Israel reminds us that this phenomenon is nothing new for just about everyone.

But Jesus challenges all of us to go deeper into the well of Divine Love and to live in God's enduring presence. Coming to an adult relationship with God means letting go of the things we hold tight to and trusting in the presence of the Lord. That lasting presence is precisely what the people of Israel forgot in the desert. That presence was the *living* water that was with them all along. From the very moment that the Lord appeared to Moses on Mount Horeb, God promised that he would be with his people. The angel of the Lord encamped with them as a great column of fire and followed them out of Egypt and led them through the Red Sea into liberation—the freedom to worship God as a people unchained. And yet their question remains: "Is the Lord in our midst or not?"

That question is carried over to the Samaritan woman Jesus encounters at Jacob's well. Like the Israelites, she is a person who needs, who wants, and who still thirsts for the presence of God. Still, Jesus asks the woman to go deeper into her own well of loneliness, to probe the depths of what she really desires—God's presence living in her midst. So Jesus tells the woman, "If you knew the gift of God and who is saying to you, 'Give me a drink,' you would have asked him and he would have given you living water." Divine Presence: That is the promise that God has provoked the woman into seeing, the reality of God himself that is often eclipsed by our own needs. The Samaritan woman's husbands are of no use to her; they are all gone. Now she is alone with Jesus at the well. So the Lord challenges her to see the gift of Divine Presence that has been disclosed right before her eyes—the living water of Christ that comes from a well that never runs dry. Jesus wants us to relax our fists and take his hand.

So our task is to recognize God's presence deep in the well of our daily lives. Our own wants and desires—whatever they may be—will lead us to discover that the real presence of Christ is right before us, in the face of our very diverse community. Nothing could be more real—or more exciting—for a baptized Christian. The living water of Christ Jesus is present within us. It is our very baptism that has transformed us into adult members of Christ's Body. We recognize the presence of the Lord in one another here and when we carry out our daily tasks. That does not matter if we are white, brown, black, or red. Baptism transforms us into the Body of Christ, where there is neither Jew nor Greek. Shall Christ's Body be divided? Baptism grants us entrance into the Holy, where there is no place for the grave sins of racism and prejudice. Baptism calls us to something different: ongoing conversion and recognition of our need for Christ and his Body.

As the *Catechism of the Catholic Church* reminds us, baptism is the door which gives us access to the other sacraments. "Baptism is the first and chief sacrament of forgiveness of sins because it unites us with Christ, who died for our sins and rose for our justification."[17] We are brought to the waters either because people of faith chose this for us as infants or because we desired it later in life. The need for baptism acknowledges that we share the sinful fate of humanity and are thirsty for justification through Christ. At every baptism, when the priest or deacon plunges the catechumen into those life-giving waters in the name of the Father, Son, and Holy Spirit, we encounter Christ in sacrament. He stands before the newly baptized saying, "You will never be thirsty again." As the Rite of Baptism makes clear, we are changed forever: "You are a new creation." We are born again, something that Jesus' friend Nicodemus could only dream of. We may find ourselves in the desert like the people of Israel or with the woman of Samaria when our own well has run dry, but as baptized Christians we know that Jesus alone can give us what we need. Our brothers and sisters present with us here in the RCIA program—catechumens awaiting that life-giving water at Easter—long for the living God and the door that opens to eternal life. We are one in Christ, healed of every division because of his passion, death, and resurrection. As Paul famously told the Galatians, "As many of you as were baptized into Christ have clothed yourselves with Christ. There is no longer Jew or Greek, there is no longer slave or free, there is no longer male and female; for all of you are one in Christ Jesus" (Gal 3:27–28). Let us accompany them to that Well of Life this Lenten season so that we might celebrate the joy of Easter together as one family in Christ.

It will undoubtedly help the preacher as interpreter to be very conscious of knowing the particulars of the congregation; these details will certainly influence his reading of the text. How will the immigrant identify with the Samaritan woman? What about the marginalized in our culture who are often excluded or ostracized like women and Samaritans in the time of Jesus? Are there members of the RCIA present? If so, they form the natural symbols in the assembly itself that work to illustrate the homily's purpose. Andrew Carl Wisdom observes how crucial it is to identify the various groups when preaching to a multi-generational assembly. Wisdom suggests that the preacher learns from high-tech marketers, who religiously monitor segmentations of the population in order to understand product receptivity.

> The marketer searches for a market. The preacher has one: the congregation. The marketer attempts to produce depth in his/her market position by effectively defining and penetrating new and diverse segments. Homilists, if they wish to pursue the opportunity, may be readily credible with varied segments as well because they are already consistently present and identified with a particular parish. Pastors must develop strategies to increase the depth of commitment in various segments of the congregation.[18]

In preaching to the multicultural assembly—or the multi-generational congregation—preachers will notice how *context will begin to shape meaning.* Contextual preaching is always necessary, but never more crucial than in a diverse congregation.

Biblical Monologist

Most of our preaching will emerge from the gifts that God has given us, and these will determine the preaching role with which we are most comfortable. Moving away from the role we have assigned for ourselves as preacher—as well as occasionally appropriating a new preaching identity—requires that we reimagine ourselves as preachers with only the Word of God as our authority. What could be more freeing? By claiming the role of interpreter, it does not mean that teaching is absent from the homily; no, the homily teaches always, but the homilist himself may be a herald, a witness, teacher, an interpreter—perhaps all four in the course of a lifetime. The Word of the Lord itself is responsible for the conversion of the People of God. At its best, preaching facilitates that Divine Word into being. To add to these four models of preaching proposed by Robert Waznak, I suggest a fifth, again one that relies on only the Word of God as our authority. And this is to occasionally become, especially in diverse congregations, a "biblical monologist." With this experiment in mind, I would like to return to my previous reference to the advantage of slipping into a "subjective point of view," one that focuses on particular characters in the biblical text for the sake of the diverse assembly.

Making the scriptures accessible for the hearer should be the pastoral work of the preacher, whether that takes place in a multicultural setting or not. The fact is that twentieth-century film culture has been negotiating a subjective interpretation of the Bible almost from the very moment light was first projected through celluloid. The centuries-old Oberammergau Passion Play, filmed before the twentieth century, would later become stories of Jesus and his disciples in the hands of D. W. Griffith, Cecil B. DeMille, and Martin Scorsese. The overwhelming success and popularity of Mel Gibson's *The Passion of the Christ* is a big hint to preachers that the living Word of God and its interpretation emerges from a variety of sources. Recently, the off-Broadway play *The Last Days of Judas Iscariot* by Stephen Adley Guirgis showed a fascinating perspective of the trial of Judas in purgatory.

These cultural texts suggest the desire of the community to see the biblical texts reframed in the context of their life situation. In a certain sense, secular film culture is giving us a clue about contextual theology by interpreting the scriptures in the twenty-first century. Indeed, the pondering of the scriptures means teasing out the way in which the biblical author has unfolded the mystery of God working within the fabric of the human drama. Monologue homilies allow the biblical characters to take on a life of their own so that the congregation might be free of any "objective" voice asserting a particular point of view. To be sure, the preacher has not entirely disappeared, since every picture of a biblical character will require some interpretation, but the monologue homily allows the preacher to disappear at least momentarily, and allow God's story to unfold in mystery and in the imagination of the listener.

The following happens to be a daily homily, but these monologues might be expanded to the Sunday context. Also, it is possible to mix a monologue with a more traditional interpretive homily, allowing the latter to provide a kind of commentary on the former.

PETER'S GATE

When I was called Simon, I first met Jesus beside the fickle waters of the Sea of Galilee. Despite myself, even then I knew he would make me see that I could fish another way—that all things were possible with God.

It happened so fast, that day when he asked us what we really thought of him. Jesus had a way of just springing things on you. He suddenly stopped in his tracks and asked us at Caesarea Philippi what people were saying about him. Well, I barely knew myself. There were fish bursting out of a net when I knew the lake was barren. There were whole limbs now that were once torn to shreds by leprosy. There was that young man formerly possessed by a demon, who is now laughing with his friends and toasting his family at Passover. All I knew of him was how he made everything new, including our ways of thinking. How could we define him when he was redefining us? Could I say he was John the Baptist or Jeremiah the prophet like the others were saying? This Jesus was no copy. All I know is that he opened gates for me and for others that used to be shut by people who thought they were holy.

The open gate. Maybe that is why I found myself with a new name and the promise of keys that day. Jesus said to me, Peter, I will give you the keys to the Kingdom of Heaven. Not that I was worthy to hold those keys or be the foundation of his Church. God knows the mistakes I made. Barely a night goes by when I don't hear that rooster screeching out my betrayal at the crack of dawn, before that terrible day. Every time I faltered, that rooster called—Peter, Peter, Peter—as if to mock the name Jesus had given me. How can one who denies him be a rock, a foundation of a Church?

Yet it somehow fit everything else he did. Jesus gave me the keys to the Kingdom, not because I was so perfect, but because he wanted me to continue to do what he himself did: to open the doors to God's infinite mercy. I will pass those keys on, not to the greatest, but to those who serve servants. I see a procession of those coming after me, some named Leo, some Gregory, some John Paul and Benedict. Whatever our name, all of us still walk through the gates owned by the one who gives us the grace to loose and to bind.

The diverse congregation is invited into prayerful dialogue with the biblical character, to imagine a context that suits their own cultural horizon. An Asian man, for instance, might have a perspective on Peter quite different from an average Westerner, since denial of a friend in some cultures is an almost unforgivable sin. Peter's monologue allows us to see a sympathetic portrait of a very human apostle. The monologue homily underlines a point I made earlier about the importance of visual preaching. The character of the monologue is *sui generis,* and the details of the life portrayed are colorful and visual, free from abstraction. To allow the congregation, quite literally, to see such a biblical piece unfolding performs a unifying moment: All are brought together by the power of visual language conjured up by the consciousness of the collective imagination. It is that collective imagination that has become the new sacred gathering-space, so to speak, during the homily. The monologue is a chance for the preacher to occasionally disengage his own ego and prejudice, and to gain new insights into diversity and the reception of the hearer. Finally, the monologue homily is also a window into the life of prayer for the preacher, who fills out the Gospel with affective meaning and contemplation by imaginative engagement with different biblical characters.

For those who do not regularly preach in a multicultural setting, the principles of diversity still apply. In a certain sense, everyone is diverse; they are culturally specific and challenged by new horizons. Learning to explore new roles and letting go of identities that rigidly identify the preacher as distinct from the congregation can only improve the breadth of the homily. Preachers should realize as well that the very diversity of multiculturalism in the assembly will itself be a cause for conversion for those who gather. Consider the attitude of the white middle-class family who find themselves hearing a homily on racial injustice sitting side by side with an African American family. Moreover, even if the congregation itself is not particularly mixed, preaching that *anticipates* diversity mirrors the larger Church and the quest for unity among God's people, drawn into the "one Body of Christ, a living sacrifice of praise…healed of all divisions."

MULTICULTURALISM
AND PREACHING JUSTICE

Although we have looked at four models of preaching, the only real example that every Christian preacher *must* follow remains Christ Jesus, who is God's Herald, the Father's Witness, the Church's Teacher, the Interpreter of the Word. When we preach like Christ, we are preaching the Word himself and making him visible. This preaching is nothing less than the cross itself, which for some will be a "stumbling block" and "foolishness," as it was for those whom Paul tried to evangelize in Corinth. Yet Jesus' cross shows us how God is in the world, the Son of Righteousness who came to take away sin and show us the compassion and mercy of the Father of all blessings. This divine love often means speaking a word of God to the powers, proclaiming justice that liberates the captive. In 1979, the U.S. Bishops released a now-celebrated statement on racism in our day, *Brothers and Sisters to Us*. In that pastoral letter, the bishops said:

> The prophetic voice of the Church, which is to be heard in every generation and even to the ends of the earth, must not be muted—especially not by the counter-witness of some of its own people. Let the Church speak out, not only in the assemblies of the bishops, but in every diocese and parish in the land, in every chapel and religious house, in every school, in every social service agency, and in every institution that bears the name Catholic. As Pope John Paul II has proclaimed, the Church must be aware of the threats to humanity and of all that opposes the endeavor to make life itself more human. The Church must strive to make every element of human life correspond to the true dignity of the human person....Therefore, let the Church proclaim to all that the sin of racism defiles the image of God and degrades the sacred dignity of human kind which has been revealed by the mystery of the Incarnation. Let all know that it is a terrible sin that mocks the cross of Christ and ridicules the Incarnation. For the brother and sister of our Brother Jesus Christ are brother and sister to us.[19]

As *Fulfilled in Your Hearing* says, the preacher is called not only to name grace, but also to acknowledge the "demons" of the community, many of which involve violations of human rights and issues of social and economic justice. These demons of racism and injustice must be courageously confronted, even as our Lord faced them in his own day. From the perspective of the homily, the difficulty with preaching justice is that there are more than a few who compartmentalize "religion" from the rest of their lives; worship is what happens on Sunday and the rest of the week it is business as usual. Broadly speaking, this attitude explains why for centuries Christians managed to rationalize slavery and, later, segregation and even eugenics. At the same time, it was the Christian abolitionists who helped bring the slave trade to an end in the nineteenth century and a Baptist preacher and other religiously minded leaders who brought civil rights to African Americans in the twentieth century. *The homily should be an integrating process of social justice for both the preacher and the congregation.* The preacher does not project a kind of religious "utopian space" that has little to do with real life. Mirroring the Incarnation, the Gospel we preach must connect with the various dimensions of everyday living. The cause for biblical justice must not only be a look backward, but also the way that the cross of Christ, God's love made real, unfolds in the contemporary world.

The clear presence of a multicultural community in the Christian assembly is an invitation to preach social justice and, indeed, corporate conversion: from a nation's hegemony that has dominated world power and its resources; from a Christian community that has participated in sinful economic and racial structures; from a model of Church that separates rather than unites. There are real heartbeats sitting out there, waiting to hear the words of peace, justice, and reconciliation. Some have experienced unimaginable difficulty in their own country. Some are political exiles. Many are separated from family and friends and face isolation, loneliness, and intense discrimination. Indeed, the congregation itself becomes the natural symbol of justice that embodies the biblical reality of God's love.

I remember working for a few summers in the Los Angeles area at a very large parish well known for its diversity—Latino, Anglos, Filipinos, African Americans. What a moving experience to celebrate the Eucharist and to see the Christian assembly reach across the aisle of this very large church and grab the hand of the person on the other side during the Our Father! That was a sign that the powers of the world needed to see, the sign of reconciliation, Christ Jesus offering himself freely to the Father. It is a vision of the Eucharist that imagines all peoples, nations, and languages together, worshiping the Lamb. *The language of the multicultural community itself articulates the realities of divine love and makes preaching the word of justice an appropriate interpretation of the Gospel.* Where else on earth but in the Eucharist could we find an eschatological sign of the Kingdom of God, a divine reality that God's future is upon all people, even as Christ offers himself to the Father on behalf of the Church?

There will be some biblical texts that naturally lend themselves to a mandate to proclaim justice. On Monday of the first week of Lent, Leviticus 19:1–2, 11–18 and Matthew 25:31–46 introduce us to Lent and the demands of justice required for true conversion. In fact, the Matthean passage suggests that, when it comes to recognizing the poor and the imprisoned, it is really a question of recognition. "Where did we see you, Lord?" is a question asked by both the sheep and the goats. And so the call for justice is also the mandate for the community to probe where charity has been lacking, not only in their own lives, but in the public, and yes, the liturgical forum as well. Again, the multicultural setting provides a marvelous symbol: The brother and sister we must recognize is the one who is "other" than me, sitting at my right hand in the gathered Church, the one I recognize as the Christ living in my midst.

It is all the more important to allow the text *and the hearer* to speak the issues of justice, so that the preacher does not use the occasion as a time for personal agenda. To be sure, everyone brings personal baggage to the ambo, but the table of the Word is a place to gather through language and not to alienate through ideological and political divisiveness. We preach the cross of Christ, not our own banners. As the late Walter Burghardt, SJ, advised:

Now in preaching the just word, we must be extraordinarily careful. Careful to preach God's word. And to preach God's word and not a word of our own making, as we have to struggle with Scripture and what it actually says to our situations....There is ever so much in social justice that is uncertain, debatable, legitimately controverted....Just how specific the Church and the preacher should be is a matter on which good and wise people can and will disagree....I can understand why many preachers will not touch justice issues with a ten-foot pole—save possibly for abortion. Still, we may not decline the call. It is not an added burden imposed by special-interest Catholics. Justice in its biblical sense is what Judaism and Christianity are all about: fidelity to God, to people, to the earth. Not to preach this is not to preach the gospel.[20]

The multicultural environment that we discover each day in and out of the worship space is a reminder that the justice that Jesus came to bring was ongoing, shaped by the roots of culture itself. There is an urgent need to face the economic, racial, and ethical justice issues in our day, some of which the congregation may experience very directly themselves. When read through the spectrum of the scriptures and the tradition of the Church, the call for justice must be a proclamation that speaks a word of comfort to the poor and the oppressed and a word of discomfort to the powerful. But always a graced word.

FOREIGN-BORN PREACHERS: SOME OBSERVATIONS AND SUGGESTIONS

We cannot neglect the multicultural issues on the other side of the ambo either: the foreign-born priest and deacon and the Anglo, English-speaking priests and deacons with whom they serve. A negative experience with a foreign-born preacher will undoubtedly affect the congregation's perception of multiculturalism and its potential gift to the Church. Seminaries and presbyterates are increasingly populated by nonnative English speakers, making the ratio of foreign priests and the established parishioners they serve a bit more challenging. As we have seen from the recommendations of countless homilists over the years, and as anyone who has preached for any length of time will tell you, a good homily emerges from the deep recesses of who we are as a person—that includes our linguistic origins as well. If you have never tried to preach in another language, then it is hard to appreciate the difficulty that foreign-born seminarians and priests face when they deliver a homily in English.

When I have nonnative English speakers in my "Introduction to the Homily" course at Saint Meinrad, I typically allow students the option of preaching in their mother tongue for the first homily (they provide written translations which they distribute to the class). Such an experience allows the seminarian or deacon to feel the vital dimension of proclamation. They preach their future homilies in English, and then the class and I give them feedback on their live performance. Later I review this homily with the student privately on their DVD recording. But not all parishes have the luxury to nurture nonnative English speakers. Foreign-born priests and deacons are usually placed in parishes without any preparation or suggestions about improving their linguistic ability.

Here is a likely scenario that has been repeated in dioceses across the country: Father Joseph is a thirty-three-year-old native of Vietnam. He came over to the United States on a religious worker visa to join his extended family and was sponsored by an older Vietnamese priest who has been living in this country for twenty years. The Diocese of St. Somewhere in the Midwest takes Fr. Joseph for five years and places him with Fr. O'Hara, an Irish American pastor in his late sixties who has a large parish. Although the parish of St. Catherine also has a thriving elementary school, Fr. Joseph is told that his responsibilities will be limited until his English improves. There is only a small Vietnamese community at St. Catherine, but Fr. Joseph spends most of his time with them and with his extended family. He finds other Vietnamese folks at the local Walmart, where many of them work in a nail-and-hair salon. When he preaches, Fr. Joseph is almost unintelligible. He does not use a text, but preaches the best he can from what he remembers from his seminary days in Vietnam. Many of the 1,500 families in the parish like Fr. Joseph and find him sincere, but they do not understand his homilies or the liturgies at which he presides. They complain to Fr. O'Hara, but with an already-unimaginably tight schedule, the pastor has little time to shepherd such foreign-born priests. Consequently, the parishioners, many of them elderly, have to deal with a mishmash of English that is endlessly frustrating. With any number of other cultural adjustments to attend to, Fr. Joseph feels alienated and unappreciated. He spends more and more time with his Vietnamese family and parishioners, actively seeking them out. His English gets worse instead of better. After five years, Fr. Joseph goes to another parish as an associate, although none of the other members of the presbyterate want to take him.

Instances like the one I have just described are not unusual and will come as no surprise to many. Indeed, the USCCB issued a statement on the topic as far back as 1999.[21] Additionally, Dean Hoge and Aniedi Okure, OP, have done an excellent job in stating the issues at stake in their book *International Priests in America: Challenges and Opportunities.* Hoge and Okure have their own long-range and short-range recommendations for international priest relations in the American Catholic Church,[22] but I would like to speculate on just three points that are closely related to preaching, some of which the Hoge/Okure Study touches on as well. What are some practical steps that parishes and diocese can take to help the preaching of non-native English-speaking priests? These are by no means exhaustive suggestions, but rather, I see these tactics as avenues to improve the quality of preaching in the immediate future.

PRACTICAL SUGGESTIONS FOR GLOBALIZING THE HOMILY

✔ *Accent reduction*

Hoge and Okure go so far as to say that "any men with weak English or extreme accents that Americans would not understand" should have their stay in the United States postponed. In any case, a standardized English test would be useful.[23] Judging from the difficulty that a multitude of parishioners have with some international priests, the use of a standardized test in English is very much in order. When it comes to preaching, perhaps the most widespread difficulty facing foreign-born homilists is their accent. I say *widespread* because even if the priest, seminarian, or deacon has been living in this country for a good while, he can still face issues concerning his accent. People in the pews report that they have difficulty understanding nonnative speakers of English. It is a problem that is becoming more prevalent, according to a story aired on NPR (National Public Radio) by Deborah Amos.[24] In her segment, "Foreign Priests Get Help Preaching in English," Amos interviewed Megan Cockram, who works at Global English Training, a Dallas-based language institute that specializes in accent reduction. Cockram suggests that many of the problems foreign priests face with their accents can be handled through "linguistic mimicry," a process that focuses on exercising new speech patterns and muscles different from those used in an individual's native tongue. In one instance, students are asked to listen to a character from the hit sitcom *Seinfeld* and choose a character's dialogue as a model for adaptation. Foreign-born priests have to be honest about their abilities and ask others for feedback; it is an opportunity for humility and conversion for the sake of preaching better.

✔ *Educate parishioners*

This process is a communal conversion. Hoge and Okure suggest that both the pastor and the parish should be prepared for the arrival of the new priest. The burden of education of our fictional Fr. Joseph at St. Catherine's should not be his alone. "Publicize the incoming priest's background, education, and talents, and meet with the laity to introduce him ahead of time. Send experts to consult with the pastor about common problems that international priests face. After the priest's arrival, sponsor welcoming meetings or mixers with parishioners and staff."[25] At the very least, St. Catherine's could be given a short article or presentation on Fr. Joseph's native country, its customs—particularly the way in which Christianity has been received there over the years. Has the newly arrived priest had a chance to tell his story outside of the liturgy? A bit more work-intensive, but certainly effective, is making available a hard copy of the homily, especially for those who have difficulty hearing. The congregation should realize that they are involved in a process, an educational revitalization of Fr. Joseph *and* themselves. If they have trouble understanding the homily, it may take some time. Feedback cards should be provided for parishioner comments on the homily. The Ladder of Preaching is an evangelistic journey partnered between the assembly and the preacher; that is all the more reason why the congregation should strive for a relationship with their new priest. There will be racial and ethnic baggage in the assembly that needs to be faced, as well as some resentments that St. Catherine's "got stuck" with "one of those foreigners" because of the vocation crunch.

Moreover, if the parishioners need to be educated, the presbyterate should be schooled in the education and background of their new member as well. I know of one diocese that had a panel of five of their foreign-born priests tell their individual stories at their yearly convocation, which met with great success. The chances are very good that, in a large diocese, many priests will not see new members or know anything about them unless they have a forum to introduce their brother priests in the midst of the presbyterate. This is also an opportunity to strive for unity in the midst of diversity.

✔ *American culture studies*

Hoge and Okure recommend a mandatory orientation program.[26] That strategy would benefit from some input by experts on American studies, a field that has been emerging in academia for decades now and is expanding in this country and abroad. International priests are often hungry for information about American history and customs. It is especially important that Fr. Joseph learn the contemporary culture of the listeners at St. Catherine's. These parishioners come from an environment with vastly different views about women, laity, and priesthood than the Vietnamese church possesses. Does Fr. Joseph have some notion of ways in which Americans communicate, or that preaching in this country has a rich history? Does Fr. Joseph, a Vietnamese native, have some notion of *American* perspectives of America's military involvement in Southeast Asia? (An excellent book for Fr. Joseph would be Tim O'Brien's very readable collection of short stories, *The Things We Carried*). Although he might find himself busy when he first gets to his new parish, Fr. Joseph might be able to enroll in a course at a local college on American culture or history, where he would be exposed to more English speakers and their local customs. Foreign-born seminarians also profit greatly from learning about American literature and film culture. These artistic representations show those from different cultures who we are as a people. The new priest should have a clear vision of those to whom he is preaching.

MISSTEPS

✗ *Failing to let go of our preconceived images of who we are as ministers*

Our roles of self-definition in a ministerial context must become secondary to the preaching of the Gospel. How have I defined myself as a priest or a deacon? Must my identity of priesthood include being someone who is set apart to teach? Or can I be flexible enough to respond to the evangelistic needs of the Church in the current cultural horizon? It is, after all, not *my* priesthood, not *my* diaconate, but the Church's. Here I want to underline what Archbishop Gregory says is our tendency to mistakenly "claim a clear role in the preaching process." Avoiding this misstep is a matter of allowing ourselves to be radically open to "the other," the Christian assembly itself, in its diverse form that allows the Word of God to reach the ears of the listener.

✕ *Failing to manage different identities as a priest with the role of preacher*

Managing different spheres of priestly identity simultaneously with the role of preacher can be difficult. All those models of preaching that I have cited earlier become exceedingly complicated when they are in competition with the two dominant roles of priesthood that have been prevalent since the 1980s—the cultic and the servant-leader models.[27] For example, if a preacher has a servant-leader model of priesthood, how does this self-understanding relate to the herald, witness, teacher, and interpreter? The servant-leader model seems closely allied to the interpreter preacher, since it states that the priest is "a leader of the community working in close collaboration with them."[28] But what if the multicultural community occasionally requires a prophetic witness?

Or, the preacher may need to assume the role of the Church-as-teacher in order to confront an aspect of a sinful world in the midst of the assembly. Can the servant-leader model integrate this unfamiliar role into the equally important self-understanding as priest?

Similarly, how is the cultic model informed by the same four categories of preaching? The cultic model, a dominant one for young priests, stresses that "the priest is essentially a man ontologically different and set apart whose job is providing the sacraments, teaching the Catholic Church's doctrine, and being a model of faith and devotion."[29] If teaching and being "set apart" are so crucial to the self-understanding of this notion of priestly identity, then how does the cultic priest as preacher become an interpreter of meaning or a contemporary herald? The cultic priest might be a stranger to actualizing the gifts of the listener, or to communicating in the contemporary world in which boundaries are less fixed. How does the cultic priest as preacher learn from his congregation?

As many others have noted, multiculturalism is a great gift to the Church, enjoining the preacher and congregation alike to hear the Word of God with compassionate ears. The diversity of the congregation—whether they be multicultural, multigenerational, or simply the fabulously rich blend within the human family—is ultimately a call to self-confrontation and conversion. Our Lord's call to preach to all nations is a summons to mission so that we might more generously hear and see the wonderful works of God in the midst of the assembly.

QUESTIONS AND PROJECTS FOR CLASS

1. Let the foreign-born students preach in their native language and provide a summary or translation in English. Ask for feedback about this experience from both the preachers and the rest of the class.

2. Ask the class to share briefly their images of priesthood (or diaconate). How does this vision of ministry incorporate multicultural ministry? What about potential conflicts? Discuss.

3. What images of preaching are there that Fr. Waznak has *not* considered? Discuss.

4. Assign the class to attend a worship service where they are a minority. Ask them to write a reflection paper on the experience.

QUESTIONS FOR REFLECTION

1. How do I experience myself as an ethnic person? What baggage and self-defenses do I bring to the preaching event? What role does culture play in my life?

2. What is my self-understanding of ordained ministry? How do models of preaching interface with this identity?

3. If English is not my native tongue, what am I doing to gain more practical skills? If English is my mother tongue, what can I do to help foreign-born priests and deacons become more integrated into the local community and diocese they serve?

4. In prayer, can I discover my cultural frame of reference and ask God to lead me to a Spirit-filled, inclusive vision of the Body of Christ?

Step Seven

CONFRONTING OBSTACLES TO EFFECTIVE PREACHING

About those preachers who, through carelessness or callousness, manage uniformly to annoy, degrade, or bore their listeners, let us say nothing more, except this: *no one sets out to preach this way!*

—James R. Nieman,
"Preaching That Drives People from the Church"[1]

In Genesis, at the end of Jacob's dream, Jacob is assured of the Divine Presence and enduring promise. The Ladder where he saw the messengers of God has brought him to a new vision: "'Surely the Lord is in this place—and I did not know it!' And he was afraid and said, 'How awesome is this place! This is none other than the house of God and this is the gate of heaven'" (Gen 28:16–17). Alan of Lille believed that the last rung on Jacob's Ladder represented allegorically the achievement of perfection in the perfect human being. The ascent from the beginning of faith to the blossoming of excellence would culminate in sharing the Word of God with others.[2] That is what preaching is all about, aptly summarized by Aquinas: "To give to others the fruits of my contemplation." In the end, preaching remains a work of pastoral charity born of prayer. As I have suggested earlier, the steps up the Ladder may have changed since the days of medieval rhetoric, but the endpoint remains the same: proclamation of the Good News to those who hear. Along the way, we share the vision of the patriarch Jacob and of Alan of Lille that evangelization will bring us and others to the gate of heaven, where the Lamb awaits us among the gathering of the blessed.

But before we make our way to that gate, we have some work to do. We might recall that Jacob's Ladder is only a stop on his larger journey; the dream yields to a contest with God and, eventually, reconciliation. Shortly after Jacob witnesses the heavenly messengers descending and ascending the Ladder, he must wrestle with a mysterious stranger, another kind of angel (Gen 32:24–32). The struggle leaves Jacob wounded but with a new name, Israel. The vision of the heavenly messengers have prepared him for this final confrontation in Peniel, because the patriarch has seen "God face to face" and survived.

In a sense, the preacher will spend a lifetime wrestling with the biblical text and discovering effective ways to preach to a changing congregation. To be prepared to face that contest, a final step is required. Step Seven is a kind of inventory of our preaching hang-ups; it is a survey and *scrutinium* of those behaviors that keep us from preaching most effectively. Such a self-check, when accurately and honestly performed, allows us to contemplate areas of growth and development. In fact, Alan of Lille himself must have thought that such self-confrontation was necessary, because he made the first rung of his own ladder "confession."[3] The implication seems to be that we cannot preach the Word of God until we have confronted our own weaknesses. But further, in my view, this last step is not only crucial for the holistic formation of preachers, but also linked by necessity to the ongoing development of ordained ministry. As the *Directory for the Life and Ministry of Priests* puts it, "The spiritual life of the priest and his pastoral ministry go hand and hand with that ongoing personal formation to deepen and harmonize the human, spiritual, intellectual and pastoral aspects of formation."[4]

Conversion happens slowly, not by gazing at one large mirror, but by viewing ourselves through the lenses of many small looking glasses. These windows are clues to the self and its progress in lifelong formation in ordained ministry. Therefore, I have structured this last step along the lines of seven small case studies, all of them, in my estimation, severe but common pitfalls in preaching. These are caricatured and exaggerated to make a point. At the same time, I have taken all of them from some version of a homily that I have seen or heard described by someone who was present for the preaching. We might find our own behavior in one or more of these, or perhaps only a slight tendency here and there. Each of these seven preaching models, or "how not to preach," are taken sequentially from the Six Sundays of Easter, Year A, and from the Ascension of the Lord. For the sake of space, they are condensed and followed by a brief reflection on each case.

THE SCATTERED PREACHER

(Easter Sunday Mass of the Day: Acts 10:34a, 37–43; Ps 118:1–2, 16–17, 22–23; Col 3:1–4; Seq Victimae Paschali Laudes; John 20:1–9)

Life is full of newness. Life is a gift. There is a reason for some of our customs. For example, we have a Christmas tree and that is always a reminder that we can share our gifts with one another, although, like Christmas, Easter is also becoming very commercialized. Just the other day I saw a television commercial for an Easter bracelet at a local jewelry store. Where is our sense of values? My mother reminded me of that question quite often. It seems like America is headed in a really bad direction. Did you

---

know that over fifty percent of couples getting married this year will be divorced before ten years are up? I hate to think that the weddings I have done are only half good. And as far as Easter is concerned, who remembers that anymore? Just a handful of loyal folks like you and me.

The disciples had a hard time remembering that Jesus promised he would rise again. Mary Magdalene wound up being the faithful friend. A true friend to Jesus. She must have remembered that he forgave her because she was a sinner. Sinners are the ones that remember. I know that converts to our faith are sometimes the ones that are the most faithful of all. The rest of us cradle Catholics take things for granted. Like Easter. I bet there are a lot of folks here who don't come to church every week. Well, that's not being very faithful, is it? How are we going to teach our children to be good religious people if we don't show them what it means to be a good Catholic? As Paul says, "Think of what is above, not of what is on earth." That means that we have to get out there and evangelize. And that is a hard thing to do, I know. But the Evangelical Church is gaining on us Catholics. They are really excited, like Mary Magdalene was about Jesus. Yet we also have to be hidden in God. Not hiding from God. Hiding in God. That means true humility. Humility to come to Mass and say we forgive one another. Even on other days than Easter, right?

So we can bring life to others, just like God gave to his Son. If we have died with him we shall also live with him.

The Problem: The homily starts out already scattered in the introduction; it has no coherent center. There is a kind of loose association of thoughts in the paragraph, moving in this direction or that. It is worth remembering that if we keep the hearer in mind, we will have less of a problem scattering thoughts. Why? *Because unlike a single person receiving a spoken message, the group hears much more slowly.* The first paragraph may work as a diary entry or even a personal reflection in a letter, but as oratory it is utterly scattered.

Also, the introduction does not lead into the first stage of the homily. That first sentence of the first stage of the homily could have been a solid beginning for a focus statement, but the text quickly devolves into a plea for people to come to church more often. This scattering occurs because of the loose associations that the Scattered Preacher makes between evangelization and church attendance. Sadly, any good observation he makes goes unheard because these sentences are buried in language that is awash with confusion. For instance, the interesting point he made about the disciples not remembering what Jesus said about his resurrection has been lost in some kind of contemporary chitchat. He "buries the lead," in journalistic terms. And the biblical quote stuck in the middle is a kind of throwaway line that is not integrated well enough. Rather than weaving the biblical text into the other threads of the homily, the scriptural text seems to just stick out like a sore thumb.

THE NARCISSISTIC PREACHER

(Second Sunday of Easter, A: Acts 2:42–47; Ps 118:2–4, 13–15, 22–24; 1 Pet 1:3–9; John 20:19–31)

[Walking up and down the aisle, the Narcissistic Preacher sings a few lines of the popular song "He touched me."]
"He touched me....He put his hands near mine and then he touched me..." Okay, I'm not in great voice

---

today. There goes my Broadway career! *[Congregation laughs.]*

I was just sitting in my living room in my cottage the other day, where I went for a few days of rest after Easter. Boy, was I tired! Holy Week and Easter are so great…but I was relaxing for a few days. I was just sitting and thinking what Thomas might have been feeling when Jesus walked into that room. That song came to my mind. It reminded me of my youth. Some would say "ill-spent" youth, but I won't go into that here, you know what I mean? *[Congregation laughs.]* When I was sitting there just praying over this Gospel, I remembered the first time I went on a date. It was my high school junior prom. And then there was that moment when you reach out and take your date's hand and *wow*! I never thought I'd be a priest after that experience, you know what I am saying, guys? *[laughter]* I felt that tingle all over. I think she felt it too, and we were just kids. But that kind of feeling is so human. Thomas must have been waiting for something like that to happen. He wanted to touch Jesus.

So Thomas has that kind of encounter with Jesus. It is really intimate. I've had those prayer experiences, and maybe you have had them too, when Jesus is so close to us. Like after I receive communion. It is like going on a date. Or when I was a little boy, my Uncle Tom (no kidding!) would come over and he would bring me a gift. He always had just a special one picked out for me. It was such a special time of growing happy and close! I really miss him now. But when I hear about Thomas in that Upper Room, I think about those days back when I'd wait at the door of our house and look for that special gift. I never knew when it was going to come. It was kind of like that for Thomas too. He did not know what was coming either. But suddenly he had a visitor. That visitor said *"Just believe."* Well, that was what my uncle was telling me too: Believe that I will always be there for you. I'll surprise you when you least expect it. It will almost seem like I am walking through walls to get there for you.

I used to be really afraid. I bet you would never guess that. But like the apostles, I was afraid a lot. People like my uncle helped me through a lot of my struggles. I remember one time I was afraid to go to gym class. I know a lot of you see me now running and playing basketball and everything. But I was a little shrimp. *[laughter]* I didn't think I could do anything. But I overcame my fear. To me, that is what our Gospel is telling us today. You know, reach out of your fears. Go for it. Jesus is there.

The Problem: The Narcissistic Preacher is unaware of the assembly and the text; it is really a moment for him to shine. Generally speaking, the preacher should avoid excessive movement if it is distracting to the congregation and not in service of the Word. If he would like to step away from the ambo, he should not travel too far; the Word of God is proclaimed there, and the homily emerges from that table. But that is the least of this preacher's compulsions. As we might expect, the Narcissistic Preacher enjoys performing—like singing. Preaching is indeed a performance, but it is for the service of proclamation for God's People. Ministry itself is fraught with trapdoors that read "It is all about me." Preaching can be one of those traps. There are very few professions that grant a more-or-less captive audience every week.

The Narcissistic Preacher quickly moves into a recollection about himself and interprets the Gospel exclusively through his own life: his Uncle Tom, his experience in prayer, his date. The Narcissistic Preacher does not have a deep faith to share with the congregation, so the Gospel reading becomes a loose exegesis applicable for daily living but filtered through a (sadly) entertaining preacher. Additionally, because of this subjectivizing approach to the homily, the assembly might as well be eavesdropping on a performer rehearsing alone, musing about the distant past. Childhood memories should be kept to a bare minimum when preaching because they will run loose, something like a wild two-year-old, and eventually overtake the scriptures. That is what happens here. The scriptures are there as a vehicle to jog the Narcissistic Preacher's memory. In that sense, he shares the company of the Scattered Preacher, because the only coherence in the homily itself is his experience and sentimental recollections. As for the congregation, they will feel little or no motivation to move into mission since the homily has been an autobiographical reflection of their preacher, more or less completely outside their own experience.

THE CROSS-LESS PREACHER

(Third Sunday of Easter, A: Acts 2:14, 22–23; Ps 16:1–2, 5, 7–11; 1 Pet 1:17–21; Luke 24:13–35)

Everyone in this assembly will recognize the name Helen Keller when I say it. Helen was born deaf and blind. It is difficult for us to imagine that world, so cut off from everything. No sense of the brightness of the sun or the sound of the wind in the trees. Evidently, she was quite the terror in her early days. Nobody could communicate to Helen. Not her parents. Not the doctors. Nobody except an exceptional teacher. Her name was Annie Sullivan. She had a breakthrough moment with her blind and deaf pupil one afternoon when Annie taught Helen how to make sense out of the world around her. It began with water. As we know, Helen went on to become a great spokesperson for our nation for people with disabilities.

Annie Sullivan found the gift in her student, much like the way Jesus was able to bring out the gifts of his disciples on the road to Emmaus. They were downcast, but he revealed himself in the breaking of the bread. They were discouraged, but he lifted them up with his word. There are so many gifted people in this parish, I am continually amazed! Some who have come through our doors never knew that they had anything to give another. But all of you made it happen. That is the gift of recognition. It is just something in the human spirit that wants to not give up on anyone. We are servants here of one another. We recognize in the Eucharist that Jesus is there for us. We may walk a lonely road, but he comes to us and opens our eyes to our own goodness. Some here may be discouraged but the Body of Christ will bring them into a new way of being. That is the Eucharist for us: food for the journey. We can continue to support each other on that road wherever it takes us. We are all a family in Christ. We are all brothers and sisters who need one another.

It may come as a surprise to you that we gave out close to five thousand meals since the First Sunday of Advent. Wow! That is practically on a parallel with Jesus and the loaves and the fishes! *[laughter]*. But that is the power of a community that recognizes one another's strengths and challenges one another's weaknesses. We are here as a community, one family, in good times and in bad.

Let us turn to this altar now where all will be fed in the breaking of the bread. We will recognize him on the road to Emmaus because he is all around us here in this church. May that same Lord who met those disciples on the road so long ago be with us now in the breaking of the bread.

The Problem: It is hard not to like the Cross-less Preacher: He is a person of good will and his homily is affirming and well organized. At the same time, though, the Cross-less Preacher, somewhat like the Scattered Preacher and the Narcissistic Preacher, does not preach through the scriptures but avoids their central message. Although many of these pitfalls in preaching often involve eisegesis, the Cross-less Preacher is one of the most obvious. If he had read and prayed over the readings thoroughly, he would have seen that Luke 24:13–35 is really about the need to interpret the scriptures through the lens of the crucified Lord. "Was it not necessary that the Christ should suffer these things and enter into his glory?"

Unfortunately, the servant-leader, adopted here as a vision of ministry, fails to be in dialogue with the readings. He misses an important doctrinal teaching-moment as well: an explanation of the theology of the passion, death, and resurrection, which would then be echoed in the Creed, professed after the homily has concluded. Jesus himself models for us the role of the preacher as interpreter when he proclaims the scriptures, "beginning with Moses and all the prophets," as referring to himself. Therefore, Jesus is mediating meaning through his passion, death, and resurrection. The homily of the Cross-less Preacher, however, resembles something of a pep talk for the parish, attempting to enliven its many gifts. In the end, the biblical readings become an occasion for a quick analogy. Even the illustration of Helen Keller/Annie Sullivan, not a bad one at all if it were integrated into an interpretation of the biblical text, remains not so much an exploration of human courage in the face of suffering as a banner-waving platform for dedicated teachers. The real difficulties and flaws of the Cross-less Preacher become evident not so much in one homily, but in the course of years. You can hold a pep rally only so often before people catch on.

More important, when the cross of Christ is empty in preaching, it leaves little room for scripture or doctrine. As we have seen earlier, the servant-leader preacher specializes in developing the gifts of the group he works with, and this facility is an enviable skill indeed. But even though we are in the season of the *Risen* Jesus, all three readings for the Third Sunday of Easter point to the cross. In Acts we must acknowledge the cross in order to witness the glory of the resurrection; in First Peter, the theological references to Christ's atonement for our sins by his passion and death are unmistakable. Clearly, the Emmaus story itself is more than an account concerning the mutual recognition of our gifts, but an awareness of the fulfillment of God's promise in offering his Son on the cross, now revealed to us in Word and Sacrament.

There are lots of doctrinal teaching-moments here for the preacher. But with a preacher who avoids the reality of the crucified God, chances are that each week's readings will be seen through the lens of a Cross-less Christ and become the occasion to have something like a parish affirmation session. That may keep the parish coffers filled, but is this preaching the Gospel? As I have suggested earlier, the preacher would do well to note how his model of priestly ministry is in dialogue with his model of preaching. Waznak's "teacher" or "interpreter" model fits nicely with this Emmaus passage, but the Cross-less Preacher cannot get beyond a shallow reading, since he is caught up in some dimension of a servant-leader priestly model. Paradoxically, if the preacher had discerned the servant-leader model more deeply, he would have learned that the servant lays down his life on the cross, rather than cheering his people on to victory.

THE TIMID PREACHER

(Fourth Sunday of Easter, A: Acts 2:14a, 36–41; Ps 23:1–6; 1 Pet 2:20b–25; John 10:1–10)

"See what love the Father has bestowed on us that we may be called the children of God."

That line from today's second reading should fill us with joy. It is love that makes us who we are if we call ourselves Christians. Remember that catchy song "They'll know that we are Christians by our love, by our love; yes, they'll know that we are Christians by our love." Those of you who are under forty won't know that song, but the rest of us will. And there is a lot of truth to that.

It is so easy to not forgive. People hurt us. We get disappointed. You know, I think if Jesus would come back to us today he would just ask, "Why can't everyone just get along?" No problem. Be happy. He brought peace with him when he came as a child in a manger. Historically speaking, that was one of the few times in the history of the world where there was a true peace, a Pax Romana. Wars have gotten us nowhere. And neither have arguments. Usually, whenever I sense some tension at a meeting or whenever conflict comes up in a discussion, I just close my eyes and say a Hail Mary. I trust that, just like Jesus, we can offer to others the other cheek. As we read in First Peter, "When he was insulted, he returned no insult; when he suffered, he did not threaten; instead, he handed himself over to the one who judges justly." That

---

is true with anything we do. Our spiritual home is in heaven, so we don't have to concern ourselves with politics. Jesus says that he is the gate. So we need to enter into our heavenly home only through him.

Let's make this a week of peace, free from conflict and division. We can know that Jesus will give us life abundantly if we walk into the gates of heaven through him alone.

The Problem: The Timid Preacher is a peace-at-all-costs homilist. As with the Cross-less Preacher, nobody is going to recoil at his message. He does not ignore the readings entirely, but they become a convenient avenue to his own agenda and eisegesis: avoiding conflict. Here, Jesus himself is brought into the picture as a support for a friction-free life. The difficulty with the Timid Preacher is that sometimes the readings demand that the homily name the demons of the community, not only its graces. In the case of John 10:1–10, it is true that Jesus is welcoming us through the gate, but there are thieves and robbers who try to get over by avoiding that sacred portal. Jesus implies that the true sheep know his voice, even though there are others who are strangers. Most important, Jesus is directing this figure of speech to the Pharisees. They are the ones that Jesus wishes to confront and he does so through the use of a masterful simile. Evidently, Jesus is preaching through confrontation himself, although doing it strategically so that each person may respond as he recognizes himself in the image.

The Timid Preacher does not want to ask the important questions of the text: Who are the Pharisees, the strangers of today, who misdirect the flock? What of those who do not enter the gate? What does it mean to recognize Jesus' voice? These queries represent potential conflict for the Timid Preacher and so he dismisses them. The Gospel passage is an invitation to justice and a commitment to Jesus and his call. The reading from Acts also suggests the firm conviction Peter has proclaimed through testimony. The fact is that the witness of the Gospel is bold and uncompromising, but the Timid Preacher cannot bear to tackle such a task. From what we can tell, the Timid Preacher avoids conflict in numerous areas in his life. He just says a Hail Mary to get through a difficult situation. There is a caveat raised in this example to remind the preacher that personal and emotional tendencies need to be kept in check when preaching in order to do service to the Word of God. If the Gospel is calling for justice, we cannot back down because it has the ring of conflict in it. God's Word is a two-edged sword.

THE KNOW-IT-ALL PREACHER

(Fifth Sunday of Easter: Acts 6:1–7; Ps 33:1–2, 4–5, 18–19; 1 Pet 2:4–9; John 14:1–12)

In the name of the Father and of the Son and of the Holy Spirit. Amen.

My dear people: Since the Second Vatican Council, there has been a lot of confusion about priesthood. You will all recognize the *priesthood of all believers* when I say that phrase. Sometimes, those who are not trained as theologians take it upon themselves to interpret this phrase as if *your* priesthood were the same as mine. Nothing could be further from the truth, my dear people. In fact, at ordination, I was given three specific tasks, which only ordained priests can accomplish through the unique status given to me by the Church in holy orders. These are preaching, teaching, and sanctifying.

As a priest, I have a responsibility to proclaim the Gospel, which is a heavy burden, to be sure. Some priests, like those who were persecuted during the Protestant Reformation in England, were tortured and executed for proclaiming the true faith. Only the ordained are able to preach since I have been ontologically changed. Spiritually, I am present with Jesus at the Last Supper every time I say the words *This is my Body. This is my Blood.* We priests are given special powers to bring the Word of God to others. It is my constant joy to stand before you each Sunday at this pulpit and announce the Good News. But secondly, I also have the gift of teaching bestowed on me by grace of ordination as well. We know that the Holy Father has a special relationship with the priests of the Church. Important documents come from Rome that need to be interpreted by the clergy in order to avoid confusion on the part of the laity. I have been specially trained in the seminary to put these in context for all the faithful, which I am happy to do. We have had so much confusion over the years and discussion about theological matters by those who have not really had much schooling in theology. Lastly, ordained priests are those who sanctify. This is the area of my priesthood that I have come to treasure so dearly, even though I have been ordained only a few years. Every day, I consecrate bread and wine into the Body and Blood of Christ. When I look at my hands, I can hardly believe that I am called to touch the sacred host of Our Lord Jesus Christ. It is such a privilege to be a priest. I thank God for it every day. I have been ontologically changed and am personally present at the Last Supper every time I say Mass.

Therefore, the one holy priesthood is really being offered here at Mass everyday as you bring your hearts to this altar. That is the priesthood of all believers gathered as I offer them up as a priest to God Our Father, who listens to my perfect prayer, the Mass. Your intentions are always close to my heart. Amen.

The Problem: The Know-It-All Preacher comes in many different characters. In this particular instance, he is an example of the young, newly ordained priest whose self-understanding of ministry is cultic and who uses this model to distance himself from the people. One of the chief ways he places a barrier between himself and the congregation is by using a deductive homily with three points and a conclusion. The homily could not be further from a process if it tried. The cultic model of priesthood tends to avoid the process of induction because this method, as I have suggested throughout this volume, encourages collaboration between the minister and the assembly. This priest is far too busy telling everyone about his own gifts to elicit gifts from the congregation. His interpretation of ordained ministry is legalistic and narrow and does not encourage what First Peter really insists on: that the assembly is being transformed into a holy priesthood by Christ himself through faith.

A liturgical homily would have been the ideal time to deepen the faith of the community, to ask them to become "living stones," as we hear in the First Letter of Peter, not to wax and wane on his own gifts through ordained ministry. The mystery of vocation could be done with teaching doctrine appropriately (such as *Christ's* priesthood), but instead, the Know-It-All Preacher uses language from the Rite of Ordination to separate himself from the faithful. He has the opposite problem of the Cross-less Preacher; the Know-It-All Preacher is not interested in eliciting any gifts from the baptized assembly. The other obvious problem here is that all of the legitimate gifts of the ordained are, ironically, *discounted* by the hearer when the preacher puts himself on a level above the congregation. An orator should never use himself as an example that makes him better than anyone else. Clearly, there are other identity issues going on with this preacher that the homily occasions.

A way into—and hopefully out of—this problem is for the priest with a cultic model of ministry to have a substantial dialogue with both the biblical text and Waznak's preaching models. The passage is asking for one of those models that this particular preacher has not yet grasped. He appears to gravitate toward the teacher preacher, but whether or not the congregation is receiving the teaching is anyone's guess. He certainly fancies himself as a teacher, but he does not do any teaching: There is no interpretation of either the scripture or genuine reflection on the doctrine that flows from these sacred texts. On the contrary, the Know-It-All Preacher pulls a line out of context and glosses it as he chooses, using deductive and reductive categories; in so doing, he reinforces his identity as a kind of teacher, but paradoxically, he empties the homily itself of substance in the process. Finally, since First Peter urges an exploration of what it means to "come close" to Jesus, the living stone, a witness preacher would be a model worth pondering as an instrument for this particular passage. At the very least, the priest who employs the cultic model for self-understanding ought to realize that there *are* other models for the interpretation of this passage. The witness model, in particular, provides an example of a priesthood that is built on testimony rather than supposed expertise, an obvious antidote to exalting one's status through ordination.

THE THERAPEUTIC PREACHER

(Sixth Sunday of Easter: Acts 8:5–8, 14–17; Ps 66:1– 7, 16, 20; 1 Peter 3:15–18; John 14:15–21)

This scene occurring in the Book of Acts in Samaria is kind of frightening, isn't it? Philip goes down to Samaria and there were apparently a lot of "unclean spirits" cry-ing out. Pretty weird. There are still a lot of people who believe in being possessed, but we might want to think about what that really is. In fact, I saw on Oprah the other day that there was someone who was claiming to be possessed. Turns out the poor woman was schizo-phrenic. I am glad we live in the twenty-first century, aren't you?

We've come a long way since those early days of the Christian Church. For a minute, I'd like every one to just close their eyes. That's right. Just sit here for a minute and breathe in that warm Spirit. Just take a deep breath. Exhale all that tension from the week. Great. *[A few moments pass.]* That feels pretty good, right? You can open your eyes now. Well, that is God working within us. Our unclean spirits are really all the stresses and harmful toxic fumes we take in all week at our work. We come here to just let it all go. We come to breathe in the Spirit and feel God's presence working deep within us. I remem-ber a few months ago I was on retreat. It was one of those times when I just could not get into the Bible because I was so preoccupied. So my retreat director told me to just be with nature all week. Notice the waves of the beach and the birds. I began to think about the Holy Spirit just blowing through the trees. It was beautiful. I began to slow down and appreciate the gift of the Spirit.

Nature is laying hands on us everyday and giving us the life-giving Spirit. It is a gift to be in the presence of some-thing so majestic and wonderful. It is good to be in the pres-ence of the Spirit wherever we go. Demons have no power over us when we notice the beauty of God all around us. Let us release the power of the Spirit on one another also, so that we all might be brothers and sisters to one another.

The Problem: The Therapeutic Preacher has a long legacy in American preaching and his influence has only increased over the years. Harry Emerson Fosdick of Riverside Church, New York City, greatly supported a preaching that was directed to a need in the congregation. Fosdick, however, usually included theological underpinnings to his "need-directed" sermons. In the Therapeutic Preacher's homily above, there is no theology and no scripture to suggest the reality of the homily's claim. In fact, the homily is a pleasant enough reflection that might be considered vaguely pantheistic. Additionally, the preacher attempts to duplicate the experience of Acts by a kind of therapeutic encounter with the congregation. That will only make some people uncomfortable, especially in large settings and with older (mostly male) congregants. Trying to accomplish the dynamic of group therapy (often very effective with about six to eight people) is risky with a large congregation. Finally, there is a real question as to whose needs are really being met in the preaching event: the preacher's or the congregation's.

One might appreciate the Therapeutic Preacher's efforts at being attentive to the coming of the Spirit. He is also fairly sensitive to the needs of the assembly and the need for prayer. But his homily functions less as a mediation of the Word of God than as an instrument for an enormous therapy group. He appears to think that the Gospel—and the Spirit—are present to serve as an antidote for worldly problems. Indeed, he tips his hand as dismissive of the Word of God when he says that on his retreat he did not seem to want to pray with the scriptures, so he had an encounter with nature instead. There is very little theological support for this language and no biblical mandate for it either. The Book of Acts is supposed to be jarring and echoes the demons that cried out when Jesus himself was present. The unrest of the "unclean spirits" suggests that the presence of the Holy is real, not simply a superstition to be dismissed along with the activity of primitives.

The Therapeutic Preacher unknowingly mimics shows like Dr. Phil where people tune in to receive, well, pop therapy. But that is not the same as hearing the Word of God, an action that the homily is supposed to effect. In the end, it is difficult to see how the faith experience of the congregation would be deepened by this kind of preaching. It would be well for the Therapeutic Preacher to look at the models of preaching discussed earlier. He really has no model. The only one he barely approaches is the interpreter, but even here it is hard to image what he is mediating except, perhaps, a séance for the late Ann Landers.

THE UNPREPARED OR
LET-ME-ENTERTAIN-YOU PREACHER

(The Ascension of the Lord: Acts 1:1–11; Ps 47:2–3, 6–9; Eph 1:17–23; Matt 28:16–20)

[*Paces up and down the aisle with hand-mike. Looks up at the ceiling.*] Did anyone see him? What must it have been like to be there when Our Lord ascended into heaven? What do *you* think it was like? [*Looks out into the congregation.*] Anybody...?

Young woman: Scary, I think. At least I would be.
Preacher: Yes, can you say *scary?* C'mon, everybody. We are talking scary!
Congregation: Scary!
Preacher: Yeah, that was what it must have been like, but somehow they would get courage from being scared. Even left alone. Isn't that something? Something that made people afraid made them unafraid. That is amazing, isn't it? What is that, everyone?
Congregation: That's amazing!
Preacher: I'll tell you what is amazing. We are going to get courage when we are scared too. It is true. Every-

body say after me now, "Jesus left us but the Spirit is coming."

Congregation: Jesus left us but the Spirit is coming!

Preacher: And what is that Spirit going to do for you? [*Looks into the congregation.*]

Older man: The Spirit is going to help my nephew in Iraq.

Preacher: Did everyone hear that? There is a lot of suffering out there and the Spirit is going to help us all. What else is the Spirit going to do? [*Walks up to a child and asks,*] "What is the Spirit going to do for you? What's your name, little girl?"

Little girl: I don't know.

Preacher: That Spirit made you a cute little girl. Anyone else?

Teenager: Help me in my school work. [*Congregation laughs.*]

Preacher: God is going to do all sorts of things for us. We just have to let him. And we are going to be afraid sometimes, but we need to take a chance, right? So let's do that this week, and just wait for that Big Guy to come down and do his thing. [*Makes the sound of the wind in the mike.*] That Spirit is going to set us free. Everybody!

Congregation: The Spirit is going to set us free!

Preacher: Again!

Congregation: The Spirit is going to set us free!

Preacher: So this is not such a scary deal after all, right? Jesus may have left us and ascended to his Father in heaven, and just like those folks in Galilee we still look up to heaven a little bit confused. But we know we are waiting for the Spirit to come down. Jesus is going to be with us always. That's a promise.

The Problem: Just when you think you have heard it all, a preacher who should have had a career on the stage in Branson, Missouri, shows up as the Unprepared Preacher. One might be tempted under such circumstances to echo the scriptures: "Who would have believed what we have heard?" Anything is possible with the Unprepared Preacher, who may be a composite of several of the previous types rolled into one (Narcissistic, Therapeutic, Scattered, Cross-less). The real difficulty is quite simple: he has nothing or very little to say but feels he wants to fill the time with something—either personal charism, laughs, or hokey material that he thinks may be worthwhile. There is much to critique here and this caricature should indicate the obvious problems, but I will mention a few that surface in similar scenarios.

Leave the talk-show format for the experts on television. Preaching the Gospel is often called to be countercultural and confrontational. That confrontational experience cannot occur if the Unprepared Preacher is mimicking a half dozen talk-show hosts who take answers from the studio audience. Don't let gadgets and technology replace the hard work of well-thought-out preaching. As we know, the liturgy is not the time to entertain the People of God, but to help them see the God of Jesus Christ who reveals salvation to his people and to help them deepen their faith with that encounter. In the above scenario, the Unprepared Preacher gestures at the action of the ascension and tries to get the congregation ready for pentecost. But what about the readings? The Gospel contains a very puzzling line: "When they saw him, they worshiped, but they doubted." What about those in the congregation who encounter this passage and need it broken open? The reality of the ascension of the Lord—an invitation to explore a central mystery of faith—is eschewed. Either for lack of preparation time, or for some other reason, the preacher moves into "Spirit language" with hopes that this will carry the day. As a result, the homily is more like a Pentecostal revival meeting that Flannery O'Connor might have conjured up. On the other hand, some of the linguistic connections are not bad (getting courage from being scared is an interesting paradox, something that a more intelligent homily would have worked through), but because the preacher is unprepared, this is a throw-away line. That strategy is not unusual for the Unprepared Preacher: He has come up with one line that he thinks works for catching the readings and builds the homily around that in a hyper, histrionic fashion. Pulling out a line here and there from the readings is not preaching; it's bluffing.

This format appears to be dialogical, but the Unprepared Preacher is really forcing the congregation to attend to him rather than the unfolding of the Word of God. This is hardly the Socratic method in action. In fact, the homily is no more narrative or inductive than any kind of late-night entertainment might be in which the audience plays a "functional" role. If this homily were a vaudeville routine, the assembly would be cast as the so-called straight man, supplying just the right answers for the more comic or funny half of the team. Audiences appear to be involved in such scenarios, but the talk-show host/preacher is really manipulating the situation into a kind of theatrical hodge-podge in which the action is mostly done by him. The hearer is left baffled in such a preaching-as-entertaining scenario. Some questions from hearers might be: How is this homily giving meaning to my life as a faithful Christian? What can the Church do for me today, anyway? Does this guy have anything to say about either the scriptures or the tradition of the Church?

Depending on the layout of the church interior, the preacher who moves about in a carefree choreography is often more obscured than he realizes from certain congregants. The ambo is there as a place for the Word to be revealed. It might say something if we are in a hurry to go elsewhere during the homily. I once concelebrated a funeral Mass of a young father who died in a tragic accident. His ten-year-old daughter, the son's classmates, and the non-Catholic mother were all together in a packed church for the Mass. After the homily was a dialogue variety like the one above. The preacher/celebrant walked around the church soliciting prayers from everyone during the General Intercessions, even asking the young daughter, "Do you have a prayer for your father? C'mon, I'm sure you do." Such moments make concele-brants and congregants alike want to crawl under the pews. Generally speaking, people do not like to be called on during the homily or at any other time during the liturgy, although there is a major exception for a youth Mass for a very prepared preacher who has a specific strategy in mind.

Similarly, technology is there for the sake of the People of God, not as an instrument to showcase an Unprepared Preacher. Gimmicks should be avoided at all costs. Props might work if the preacher knows how to use them well and they *intentionally* illustrate a point or perspective. From the point of view of deliv-ery, few things are more important than learning to use the microphone well. Sound systems are crucial for the listeners. Preachers should realize that real performers—those who are interested in actualizing a text in the experience of the hearer or spectator—are very professional when it comes to learning about sound. But most preachers would not know the difference between an omnidirectional and a unidirectional microphone. This is the real point of technology: not gadgets that might enter-tain the congregation, but instruments that make the experience of worship an effective process for the sake of the hearer.

The Unprepared Preacher would be advised to return to the Ladder of Preaching at the first step and spend some time with the scriptures in silent awe. Indeed, much of the problems that occur in the course of these homiletic case studies could have been avoided if the preacher paid careful attention to praying, studying the scripture, developing a homiletic method for the hearer, and discovering the culture of the congregation. Additionally, as I have intimated earlier, the preaching models proposed by Robert Waznak are a very useful checkpoint to discover the core of the preaching event—or the lack of it. Clearly, the Unprepared Preacher is not only lacking any engagement with the text, but he has no sense of what the theological function of preaching entails—as herald, witness, teacher, or interpreter. The same may be said of the other preaching pitfalls characterized in this last step: they lack the foundational ground and self-reflection so crucial to preaching in the liturgical assembly.

FEEDBACK FROM THE ASSEMBLY

As a final coda to this run up the Ladder of Preaching, let me suggest the use of feedback. The first kind of self-confrontation in the pulpit is a video/DVD recording of the preaching event. Preachers are often amazed at what bad habits they have picked up over the years when they see themselves on tape. It is now standard for teachers of homiletics to use such feedback in the classroom.

The absolute foolproof method of confronting any homiletic problem is information about the preaching event gleaned from the congregation, something very few preachers are willing to risk. Who, after all, wants to hear that 80 percent of the people did not hear the focus statement, or that there just was no focus at all? And yet the only way for a preacher to see a problem is by asking what was heard. The further advantage of asking the congregation for feedback is that these questions show that the preacher is really interested in serving the Word of God. The practice of asking even just a few questions on a card distributed at the end of the liturgy allows the congregation to say that the time for the homily is important. The baptized assembly needs to take ownership of their role as listeners. That may be a fairly threatening prospect to poor preachers, but the courageous homilist will want to teach the assembly how to listen for the sake of the Kingdom of God, which breaks through in proclamation. Can preachers train the congregation how to listen and take responsibility for hearing? I believe that the answer is yes. As Paulist Father Robert Rivers has argued, "Today, there is a growing realization that in order to make any substantial progress in any one parish activity, such as adequate catechesis, it is necessary to take a more holistic approach that is rooted in the wider activities of the entire parish....Why shouldn't the entire parish hold itself accountable for improving the quality for the preaching experience?"[5] After a well-developed preacher, the conscientious formation of the listener is the best way to improve homilies. We need to educate the assembly about how to be good listeners and then how to demand more from their preachers. This education might be done in RCIA groups, parish missions, or scriptural reflections. The question for the preacher of a challenging congregation is a daunting one, but it is a dialogue that will always find him on Holy Ground.

SAMPLE FEEDBACK QUESTIONS FOR A TYPICAL CONGREGATION

In one sentence, can you say what you heard? _____
_____
_____

Did the preacher use the biblical readings for the day well? _____
_____

The homily motivated me to _____
_____
_____.

The homily did not really motivate me. I felt it _____
_____
_____.

The delivery of the homilist was:
☐ excellent   ☐ good   ☐ needs to improve
_____
_____

NOTES

Step One

1. Quoted in *America*, vol. 198, No. 7 (March 3, 2008), 7.

2. *Pontificale Romanum / De ordinatione Episcopi, Presbyterorum et Diaconorum*, cap. II, n. 151, *Ed. Typical altera* 1990, 87–88.

3. St. Augustine, *Teaching Christianity: De Doctrina Christiana*, trans. Edmund Hill, OP, ed. John E. Rotelle, OSA (New Hyde Park, NY: New City Press, 1996), 218.

4. John of the Cross, *The Collected Works of St. John of the Cross*, trans. Kieran Kavanaugh, OCD, and Otilio Rodriguez, OCD (Washington, DC: ICS Publications, 1991), 348.

5. Pope Benedict XVI (Joseph Ratzinger), *Jesus of Nazareth: From the Baptism in the Jordan to the Transfiguration* (New York: Doubleday, 2007), 7.

6. *Gaudium et Spes*, *The Documents of Vatican II*, ed. Walter Abbottt, SJ (Piscataway, NJ: New Century, 1966), 198–99.

7. *Sacrosanctum Concilium*, *The Documents of Vatican II*, 140.

8. Gregory the Great, *The Book of Pastoral Rule*, in Richard Lischer, ed., *The Company of Preachers: Wisdom on Preaching* (Grand Rapids, MI, and Cambridge: Eerdmans, 2002), 356.

9. Alan of Lille, *The Art of Preaching*, trans. Guillian R. Evans (Kalamazoo, MI: Cistercian Publications, 1981), 17.

10. Maximus the Confessor, "From the Five Hundred Chapters by Saint Maximus the Confessor," in *Liturgy of the Hours*, Vol. I (New York: Catholic Book Publishing, 1975), 519.

11. Congregation for the Clergy, *Directory on the Ministry and Life of Priests* (Vatican City: Libreria Editrice Vaticana, 1994), 45–46.

12. Congregation for the Clergy, *Directory*, 48.

13. Blessed Mother Teresa of Calcutta, "Jesus, the Word to Be Spoken," in *Magnificat* (Yonkers, NY: Magnificat/Martha Publishing, 2008), 111.

14. John Henry Newman, "University Preaching," in Lischer, *The Company of Preachers*, 382.

15. Newman, 383.

16. Newman, 383.

17. *Gaudium et Spes, The Documents of Vatican II*, 246.

18. *Sacrosanctum Concilium, The Documents of Vatican II*, 141.

19. *Presbyterorum ordinis, The Documents of Vatican II*, 539.

20. NCCB, *Fulfilled in Your Hearing: The Homily in the Sunday Assembly* (Washington, DC: U.S. Catholic Conference, 1982), 4.

21. NCCB, *Fulfilled in Your Hearing*, 4, 7.

22. *Fulfilled in Your Hearing*, 10.

23. Ron Knott, "Teaching Spiritual Leadership," in *Seminary Journal*, vol. 13. no 1 (Spring 2007), 32.

24. Thomas Merton, *New Seeds of Contemplation* (New York: New Directions, 1961), 64.

25. Elizabeth Barrett Browning, *Aurora Leigh*, in *The Poetical Works of Elizabeth Barrett Browning* (New York: MacMillan, 1987), 466; see also Robert Waznak, *Introduction to the Homily* (Collegeville, MN: Liturgical Press, 1998), 55.

26. "A Parishioner" and "Our Broken Parish," in *America*, 198 (4): February 11, 2008, 25.

Step Two

1. *Dei Verbum, The Documents of Vatican II*, 125.

2. *Dei Verbum*, 127.

3. NCCB, *Fulfilled in Your Hearing*, 18, 19.

4. Stephen Prothero, *Religious Literacy: What Every American Needs to Know—and Doesn't* (San Francisco: HarperCollins, 2007), 6

5. NCCB, *Fulfilled in Your Hearing*, 18.

6. Ronald Rolheiser, *The Holy Longing: The Search for a Christian Spirituality* (New York: Doubleday, 1999), 231.

7. Alan of Lille, 21.

8. *Dei Verbum, The Documents of Vatican II*, 127.

9. NCCB, *Fulfilled in Your Hearing*, 21.

10. The Pontifical Biblical Commission, *The Interpretation of the Bible in the Church* (Boston: Pauline Media, 1993), 29.

11. *The Interpretation of the Bible in the Church*, 93.

12. *The Interpretation of the Bible in the Church*, 90.

13. Pope Benedict XVI, *Jesus of Nazareth*, 121–22.

14. *The Interpretation of the Bible in the Church*, 74.

15. Bernhard W. Anderson, *The Unfolding Drama of the Bible*, 4th ed. (Minneapolis: Fortress Press, 2006).

16. Raymond E. Brown, *The Gospel According to John I–XII* (New York: Doubleday, 1966), 165.

17. Frank J. Matera, *Strategies for Preaching Paul* (Collegeville, MN: Liturgical Press, 2001), 3.

18. *Sacrosanctum Concilium*, Abbott, 155.

19. Ardith Spierling Hayes, "Homiletics in a New Context," *Preaching the Story*, eds. Edmund A. Steimle, Morris J. Niedenthal, and Charles L. Rice (Philadelphia: Fortress Press, 1980), 196.

20. Nathan Mitchell, "Symbols are Actions, Not Objects," *Living Worship* 13, no. 2 (February 1977), 1.

21. See, Edward Foley, OFM Cap, "The Homily Beyond Scripture: *Fulfilled in Your Hearing* Revisited," *Worship* 73 (1999): 351–58.

22. *Sacrosanctum Concilium*, Abbott, 141.

23. John Allyn Melloh, SM, "On the Vocation of the Preacher," *Ars Liturgiae: Worship, Aesthetics and Praxis; Essays in Honor of Nathan D. Mitchell*, ed. Clare V. Johnson (Chicago: Liturgical Training Publications, 2003), 172–73.

24. Martin Connell, *Eternity Today: On the Liturgical Year*, vol. 1 (New York and London: Continuum, 2006), 4.

25. Mark Searle, "Sunday: The Heart of the Liturgical Year," *Between Memory and Hope: Readings on the Liturgical Year*, ed. Maxwell E. Johnson (Collegeville, MN: Liturgical Press, 2000), 74.

26. Connell, *Eternity Today*, 3–4.

27. James A. Wallace, CSsR, *Preaching to the Hungers of the Heart: The Homily on the Feasts and within the Rites* (Collegeville, MN: Liturgical Press, 2002), 32.

28. Wallace, *Preaching to the Hungers of the Heart*, 78.

29. Wallace, *Preaching to the Hungers of the Heart*, 113.

30. NCCB, *Fulfilled in Your Hearing*, 24.

Step Three

1. Ken Untener, *Preaching Better: Practical Suggestions for Homilists* (New York/Mahwah, NJ: Paulist Press, 1999), 44.

2. St. Augustine, *Teaching Christianity*, 203.

3. James R. Nieman, "Preaching That Drives People from the Church," in *A Reader on Preaching: Making Connections*, ed. David Day, Jeff Astley, and Leslie J. Francis (Burlington, VT: Ashgate, 2005), 251.

4. NCCB, *Fulfilled in Your Hearing*, 24.

5. Ronald Allen, "Simple Inductive Preaching," in *Patterns of Preaching: A Sermon Sampler*, ed. Ronald Allen (St. Louis, MO: Chalice Press, 1998), 64.

6. Fred B. Craddock, *Overhearing the Gospel*, rev. ed. (St. Louis, MO: Chalice Press, 2002), 104.

7. John of the Cross, *The Collected Works*, 349.

8. Thomas G. Long, *The Witness of Preaching*, 2nd ed. (Louisville, KY: Westminster John Knox, 2005), 137.

9. Long, *The Witness of Preaching*, 137.

10. Long, *The Witness of Preaching*, 137.

11. Long, *The Witness of Preaching*, 137.

12. Fred B. Craddock, *Preaching* (Nashville, TN: Abingdon Press, 1985), 147–48.

13. Ken Untener, *Preaching Better*, 42.

14. Untener, *Preaching Better*, 43.

15. Untener, *Preaching Better*, 43.

16. Untener, *Preaching Better*, 44.

17. Untener, *Preaching Better*, 44.

18. Stephen V. DeLeers, *Written Text Becomes Living Word: The Vision and Practice of Sunday Preaching* (Collegeville, MN: Liturgical Press, 2004), 107–8.

19. The other characteristics are personal, liturgical, and inculturated. See *Written Text Becomes Living Word*, 55–101.

20. For the example mentioned in my homily, see Flannery O'Connor, "The River," in *The Complete Stories* (New York: Farrar, Straus and Giroux, 1971).

21. For a fuller exposition of this, see Guerric DeBona, OSB, "Preaching for the Plot," *New Theology Review* (February 2001): 14–22.

22. Mary Catherine Hilkert, OP, *Naming Grace: Preaching and the Sacramental Imagination* (New York: Continuum, 1997), 99.

23. Robert P. Waznak, SS, *Like Fresh Bread: Sunday Homilies in the Parish* (New York and Mahwah, NJ: Paulist Press, 1993), 55–56.

24. E. M. Forster, *Aspects of the Novel* (New York: Harcourt Brace and World, 1955), 86.

Step Four

1. St. Francis de Sales, *On the Preacher and Preaching*, trans. John K. Ryan (Chicago: Henry Regnery Company, 1964), 52–53.

2. Paul Scott Wilson, *The Four Pages of the Sermon: A Guide to Biblical Preaching* (Nashville, TN: Abingdon Press, 1999), 13.

3. NCCB, *Fulfilled in Your Hearing*, 28.

4. This section is based in part on my more detailed survey of Buttrick's method. See Guerric DeBona, OSB, *Fulfilled in Our Hearing: History and Method of Christian Preaching* (New York and Mahwah, NJ: Paulist Press, 2005), 55–71.

5. Fred Craddock, *As One Without Authority* (St. Louis, MO: Chalice Press, 2001), 64–65.

6. Richard Eslinger, *The Web of Preaching* (Nashville, TN: Abingdon Press, 2003), 139.

7. David Buttrick, *Homiletic: Moves and Structures* (Philadelphia: Fortress Press, 1987), 451.

8. Allen, *Patterns of Preaching*, 89.

9. Buttrick, *Homiletic*, 35, 45.

10. Ronald Rolheiser, *Forgotten Among the Lilies: Learning to Love Beyond Our Fears* (New York: Doubleday, 2005), 6.

11. Eugene L. Lowry, *The Homiletic Plot*, rev. ed. (Louisville, KY: Westminster John Knox Press, 2001), 54.

12. Wilson, *The Four Pages*, 27.

13. Wilson, *The Four Pages*, 38.

14. William Levada, "The Homilist: Teacher of the Faith," *Origins* 37, no. 38 (March 6, 2008): 605.

15. Levada, "The Homilist," 605.

16. Wilson, *The Four Pages*, 48.

17. Wilson, *The Four Pages*, 51.

18. Wilson, *The Four Pages*, 79.

19. See Wilson, *The Four Pages*, 59–67.

20. See Wilson, *The Four Pages*, 209–12.

Step Five

1. Kerry Patterson, Joseph Grenny, Ron McMillan, and Al Switzler, *Crucial Confrontations: Tools for Resolving Broken*

Promises, Violated Expectations, and Bad Behavior (New York: McGraw-Hill, 2005), 113.

2. See DeBona, *Fulfilled in Our Hearing*, 20–23.

3. J. Randall Nichols, "Communication," in *A Concise History of Preaching*, ed. William H. Willimon and Richard Lischer (Louisville, KY: Westminster John Knox Press, 1995), 85.

4. Paul VI, "On Evangelization in the Modern World" (*Evangelii Nuntiandi*) (Boston: Pauline, 1975), 26.

5. John Paul II, "The Church in America" (*Ecclesia in America*) (Boston: Pauline, 1999), 115.

6. Augustine, *Teaching Christianity*, 202.

7. Pontifical Council for Culture, *Toward a Pastoral Approach to Culture* (Boston: Pauline, 1999), 28–29.

8. See Levada, "The Homilist: Teacher of the Faith," 605–6.

9. Chip Heath and Dan Heath, *Made to Stick: Why Some Ideas Survive and Others Die* (New York: Random House, 2007), 9.

10. NCCB, *Fulfilled in Your Hearing*, 4.

11. Heath and Heath, *Made to Stick*, 16.

12. Heath and Heath, *Made to Stick*, 30.

13. Heath and Heath, *Made to Stick*, 41.

14. Heath and Heath, *Made to Stick*, 48.

15. Heath and Heath, *Made to Stick*, 62.

16. Heath and Heath, *Made to Stick*, 16.

17. Heath and Heath, *Made to Stick*, 69.

18. James A. Wallace, Robert P. Waznak, and Guerric DeBona, *Lift Up Your Hearts: Homilies and Reflections for the "C" Cycle* (New York and Mahwah, NJ: Paulist Press, 2006), 72.

19. Heath and Heath, *Made to Stick*, 17.

20. Heath and Heath, *Made to Stick*, 99–100.

21. Anne Lamott, *Bird by Bird: Some Instructions on Writing and Life* (New York: Doubleday/Anchor, 1994), 100.

22. Quoted in Lamott, *Bird by Bird*, 100.

23. Heath and Heath, *Made to Stick*, 105.

24. James A. Wallace, *Imaginal Preaching: An Archetypal Perspective* (New York and Mahwah, NJ: Paulist Press, 1995), 19.

25. Heath and Heath, *Made to Stick*, 156.

26. Heath and Heath, *Made to Stick*, 157.

27. Thomas G. Long, "Telling the Truth about Death and Life: Preaching at Funerals," *Journal for Preachers* (Easter 1997): 3–12.

28. Levada, "The Homilist: Teacher of the Faith," 605.

29. Heath and Heath, *Made to Stick*, 18.

30. Quoted in Heath and Heath, *Made to Stick*, 165.

31. See Heath and Heath, *Made to Stick*, 197 ff.

32. Heath and Heath, *Made to Stick*, 203.

33. Heath and Heath, *Made to Stick*, 18.

34. See Heath and Heath, *Made to Stick*, 218–19.

35. Heath and Heath, *Made to Stick*, 222–23.

36. Heath and Heath, *Made to Stick*, 226.

37. Heath and Heath, *Made to Stick*, 229.

Step Six

1. See Mark O'Keefe, OSB, *In Persona Christi: Reflections on Priestly Identity and Holiness* (St. Meinrad, IN: Abbey Press, 1998), 27. In addition to conversion, O'Keefe identifies gratitude and commitment as the dispositions growing up in the priestly calling.

2. See DeBona, "Multicultural Preaching," in DeBona, *Fulfilled in Our Hearing*, 125–67.

3. Quoted in DeBona, *Fulfilled in Our Hearing*, 125.

4. For a brief recounting of the hermeneutic involved with African American preaching, see DeBona, *Fulfilled in Our Hearing*, 131–42.

5. Archbishop Wilton Gregory, "Preaching in the Multicultural Context of the U.S." The Carl J. Peter Lecture, January 13, 2008, at the North American College, Rome, reprinted in *Origins* 37, no. 33 (January 31, 2008), 524.

6. Gregory, "Multicultural Preaching," 524–25.

7. Gregory, "Multicultural Preaching," 525.

8. Robert Waznak, *Introduction to the Homily* (Collegeville, MN: Liturgical Press, 1998), 33.

9. Quoted in Waznak, *Introduction to the Homily*, 39.

10. Quoted in Waznak, *Introduction to the Homily*, 61.

11. See Anna Carter Florence, *Preaching as Testimony* (Louisville, KY: Westminster John Knox Press, 2007).

12. Waznak, *Introduction to the Homily*, 66.

13. Gregory the Great, *The Book of Pastoral Rule*, in *The Company of Preachers: Wisdom on Preaching, Augustine to the Present*, ed. Richard Lischer (Grand Rapids/Cambridge: Eerdmans, 2002), 356–57.

14. NCCB, *Fulfilled in Your Hearing*, 25, and quoted in Waznak, 53.

15. Quoted in Waznak, *Introduction to the Homily*, 52.

16. Levada, "The Homilist: Teacher of the Faith," 605.

17. *Catechism of the Catholic Church*, 2nd ed. (Washington, DC: United States Catholic Conference, 1994), 867.

18. Andrew Carl Wisdom, *Preaching to a Multi-Generational Assembly* (Collegeville, MN: Liturgical Press, 2004), 51.

19. NCCB, *Brothers and Sisters to Us: U.S. Bishops' Pastoral Letter on Racism in Our Day* (Washington, DC: USCC, 1979), 8–9.

20. Walter J. Burghardt, SJ, *Let Justice Roll Down Like Waters: Biblical Justice Homilies Throughout the Year* (New York and Mahwah, NJ: Paulist Press, 1998), 13.

21. USCCB, *Guidelines for Receiving Pastoral Ministers* (Washington, DC: USCCB, 1999).

22. Dean R. Hoge and Aniedi Okure, *International Priests in America: Challenges and Opportunities* (Collegeville, MN: Liturgical Press, 2006), 123–24.

23. Hoge and Okure, *International Priests*, 124.

24. Deborah Amos, "Foreign Priests Get Help Preaching in English," National Public Radio, aired on October 9, 2007. See http://www.npr.org/templates/story/story.php?storyId=15111020.

25. Hoge and Okure, *International Priests*, 124.

26. Hoge and Okure, *International Priests*, 124.

27. See Dean R. Hoge, *Experiences of Priests Ordained Five to Nine Years: A Study of Recently Ordained Catholic Priests* (Collegeville, MN: Liturgical Press, 2006), 59–71.

28. Hoge, *Experiences of Priests*, 59.

29. Hoge, *Experiences of Priests*, 59.

Step Seven

1. James R. Nieman, "Preaching That Drives People from the Church," in *A Reader on Preaching* (Burlington, VT: Ashgate, 2005), 248.

2. Alan of Lille, *The Art of Preaching*, 15.

3. Alan of Lille, *The Art of Preaching*, 15.

4. Congregation for the Clergy, *Directory for the Life and Ministry of Priests*, 76.

5. Robert S. Rivers, CSP, "Preaching Too Important to Be Left to Preachers?" *Chicago Studies*, vol. 44, no. 3 (Fall/Winter 2005).

BIBLIOGRAPHY

Abbott, William, SJ, ed. *The Documents of Vatican II*. New Brunswick, NJ: New Century Press, 1966.

Allan of Lille. *The Art of Preaching*. Trans. G. R. Evans. Cistercian Studies Series 23. Kalamazoo, MI: Cistercian Publications, 1981.

Allen, Ronald J. *Patterns of Preaching*. St. Louis: Chalice Press, 1998.

Anderson, Bernhard W. *The Unfolding Drama of the Bible*. 4th ed. Minneapolis: Fortress Press, 2006.

Babin, Pierre, OMI, and Mercedes Iannone. *The New Era in Religious Communication*. Minneapolis: Fortress Press, 1991.

Bausch, William J. *Story Telling the Word: Homilies and How to Write Them*. Mystic, CT: XXIII, 1996.

Bevans, Stephen. *Models of Contextual Theology*. Maryknoll, NY: Orbis, 1992.

Burghardt, Walter, SJ. *Let Justice Roll Down Like Waters: Biblical Justice Homilies Throughout the Year*. New York/Mahwah, NJ: Paulist Press, 1997.

———. *Preaching: The Art and the Craft*. New York/Mahwah, NJ: Paulist Press, 1987.

Burke, John, OP, and Thomas P. Doyle, OP. *The Homilist's Guide to Scripture, Theology and Canon Law*. New York: Pueblo, 1986.

Buttrick, David. *Preaching the New and the Now*. Louisville: WJK, 1998.

———. *A Captive Voice: The Liberation of Preaching*. Louisville: WJK, 1994.

———. *Homiletic: Moves and Structures*. Philadelphia: Fortress Press, 1987.

Catechism of the Catholic Church, 2nd ed. Washington, DC: United States Catholic Conference, 1994.

Chrysostom, St. John. *The Priesthood*. Trans. W. A. Jurgens. New York: MacMillan, 1955.

Climacus, John. *The Ladder of Divine Ascent*. New York/Mahwah, NJ: Paulist Press, 1982.

Code of Canon Law: Latin-English Edition. Washington, DC: Canon Law Society of America, 1983.

Congregation for the Clergy. *Directory on the Ministry and Life of Priests*. Vatican City: *Libreria Editrice Vaticana*, 1994.

Connell, Martin. *Eternity Today: On the Liturgical Year*, Vol. 1. New York and London: Continuum, 2006.

Craddock, Fred B. *As One Without Authority*. St. Louis: Chalice Press, 2001.

———. *The Cherry Log Sermons*. Louisville: WJK, 2001.

———. *Luke*. Louisville: WJK, 1990.

———. *Preaching*. Nashville: Abingdon Press, 1985.

———. *Overhearing the Gospel*. Nashville: Abingdon Press, 1978.

Crawford, Evans E., and Thomas Troeger. *The Hum: Call and Response in African American Preaching*. Nashville: Abingdon Press, 1995.

Davis, Kenneth G., OFM Conv, and Jorge L. Presmanes, eds. *Preaching and Culture in Latino Congregations*. Chicago: LTP, 2000.

Day, David, Jeff Astley, and Leslie J. Francis. *A Reader on Preaching: Making Connections*. Burlington, VT: Ashgate, 2005.

DeBona, Guerric, OSB. "Preaching for the Plot." *New Theology Review* 14, no. 1, 2001: 14–22.

———. *Fulfilled in Our Hearing*. New York/Mahwah, NJ: Paulist Press, 2006.

DeLeers, Stephen V. *Written Text Becomes Living Word: The Vision and Practice of Sunday Preaching*. Collegeville, MN: Liturgical Press, 2004.

———. "The Place of Preaching in the Ministry and Life of Priests." In *The Theology of Priesthood*, eds. Donald J. Goergen and Ann Carido. Collegeville, MN: Liturgical Press, 2000: 87–103.

DeSales, Francis. *On the Preacher and Preaching*. Trans. John K. Ryan. Chicago: Henry Regnery Company, 1964.

Edwards, O. C. *A History of Preaching*. Nashville: Abingdon Press, 2004.

———. *Elements of Homiletic: A Method for Preparing to Preach*. New York: Pueblo, 1982.

Elliot, Mark Barger. *Creative Styles of Preaching*. Louisville: WJK, 2000.

Eslinger, Richard L. *The Web of Preaching*. Nashville: Abingdon Press, 2002.

———. *A New Hearing*. Nashville: Abingdon Press, 1987.

Florence, Anna Carter. *Preaching as Testimony*. Louisville, KY: Westminster John Knox Press, 2007.

Foley, Edward, OFM Cap. "The Homily Beyond Scripture: *Fulfilled in Your Hearing* Revisited." *Worship* 43, no. 4 (July 1999): 352–58.

Grasso, Dominic, SJ. *Proclaiming God's Message: A Study in the Theology of Preaching*. Notre Dame, IN: Notre Dame Press, 1965.

Gregory, Wilton. "Preaching in the Multicultural Context of the U.S." *Origins* 37, no. 33 (January 31, 2008): 521–27.

Heath, Chip, and Dan Heath. *Made to Stick: Why Some Ideas Survive and Others Die*. New York: Random House, 2007.

Hilkert, Mary Catherine. *Naming Grace: Preaching and the Sacramental Imagination*. New York: Continuum, 1997.

Hoge, Dean R. *Experiences of Priests Ordained Five to Nine Years: A Study of Recently Ordained Catholic Priests*. Collegeville, MN: Liturgical Press, 2006.

Hoge, Dean R., and Aniedi Okure. *International Priests in America: Challenges and Opportunities*. Collegeville, MN: Liturgical Press, 2006.

Janowiak, Paul. *The Holy Preaching: The Sacramentality of the Word in the Liturgical Assembly.* Collegeville, MN: Liturgical Press, 2000.

Jensen, Richard A. *Thinking in Story.* Lima, OH: CSS Press, 1993.

Jeter, Joseph L., and Ronald J. Allen. *One Gospel, Many Ears: Preaching for Different Listeners in the Congregation.* St. Louis: Chalice Press, 2002.

John Paul II, Pope. *The Church in America: Post-Synodal Apostolic Exhortation.* Boston: Pauline Books, 1999.

———. *Pastores Dabo Vobis.* Washington, DC: USCCB, 1992.

LaMott, Anne. *Bird by Bird: Some Instructions on Writing and Life.* New York: Doubleday/Anchor, 1994.

Levada, William. "The Homilist: Teacher of the Faith." *Origins* 37, no. 38 (March 6, 2008): 602–8.

Lischer, Richard, ed. *The Company of Preachers: Wisdom on Preaching, Augustine to the Present.* Grand Rapids: Eerdmans, 2002.

Long, Thomas G. "Telling the Truth about Death and Life: Preaching at Funerals." *Journal for Preachers* (Easter 1997), 3–12.

———. *The Witness of Preaching.* Louisville: Westminster John Knox Press, 1990.

———. *Preaching and the Literary Forms of the Bible.* Philadelphia: Fortress Press, 1989.

Lowry, Eugene. *Doing Time in the Pulpit: The Relationship Between Narrative and Preaching.* Nashville: Abingdon Press, 1989.

———. *How to Preach a Parable.* Nashville: Abingdon, 1989.

———. *The Homiletic Plot,* rev. ed. Louisville: Westminster John Knox Press, 2001.

Matera, Frank J. *Strategies for Preaching Paul.* Collegeville, MN: Liturgical Press, 2001.

Melloh, John Allyn, SM. "On the Vocation of the Preacher." *Ars Liturgiae: Worship, Aesthetics and Praxis.* Ed. Claire V. Johnson. Chicago: LTP, 2003, 161–90.

Meyers, Robin R. *With Ears to Hear: Preaching as Self-Persuasion*. Cleveland: Pilgrim Press, 1993.

Mitchell, Henry. *Black Preaching: The Recovery of a Powerful Art*. Nashville: Abingdon Press, 1991.

NCCB. *Sunday Celebration in the Absence of a Priest*. Washington, DC: USCC, 1996.

————. *Fulfilled in Your Hearing*. Washington, DC: USCC, 1982.

————. *Brothers and Sisters to Us: U.S. Bishops' Pastoral Letter on Racism in Our Day*. Washington, DC: USCC, 1997.

————. *Many Pilgrims One Family of God: A Parish Multicultural Resource Manual*. Washington, DC: USCC, 1992.

Nieman, James R., and Thomas G. Rogers. *Preaching to Every Pew: Cross-Cultural Strategies*. Minneapolis: Fortress Press, 2001.

Organ, Deborah. "Immigrants and Inculturation." *America* 189, no. 15 (November 10, 2003): 12–14.

Paul VI, Pope. "On Evangelization in the Modern World," *Evangelii Nuntiandi*. Boston: Pauline, 1975.

Pontifical Biblical Commission. *The Interpretation of the Bible in the Church*. Boston: Pauline Media, 1993.

Power, David, OMI. *"The Word of the Lord": Liturgy's Use of Scripture*. Maryknoll, NY: Orbis, 2001.

Prothero, Stephen. *Religious Literacy: What Every American Needs to Know—and Doesn't*. San Francisco: HarperCollins, 2007.

Rahner, Karl, SJ, ed. *The Renewal of Preaching: Theory and Practice*. New York: Paulist Press, 1968.

Ratzinger, Joseph (Pope Benedict XVI). *Jesus of Nazareth: From the Baptism in the Jordan to the Transfiguration*. New York: Doubleday, 2007.

Rivers, Robert S., CSP. "Preaching Too Important to Be Left to Preachers?" *Chicago Studies* 44, no. 3 (Fall/Winter, 2005): 263–72.

————. *Jesus: Symbol Maker for the Kingdom*. Minneapolis: Augsburg Fortress Press, 1981.

Skudlarek, William. *The Word in Worship: Preaching in a Liturgical Context*. Nashville: Abingdon Press, 1981.

Sloyan, Gerard S. *Preaching from the Lectionary: An Exegetical Commentary*. Minnesota: Augsburg Fortress Press, 2003.

———. "Some Thoughts on Liturgical Preaching." *Worship* 71, no. 5 (September, 1997): 386–99.

———. *Worshipful Preaching*. Philadelphia: Fortress Press, 1984.

Stackhouse, Max L., Tim Dearborn, and Scott Paeth, eds. *The Local Church in a Global Era: Reflections for a New Century*. Grand Rapids: Eerdmans, 2000.

Steimle, Edmund A., Morris J. Niedenthal, and Charles Rice. *Preaching the Story*. Philadelphia: Fortress Press, 1980.

Stern, Richard C. "Preaching as Listening: Good Preachers Listen First." *Church* (Winter 1999): 21–26.

———. *Preaching for Today and Tomorrow* (handbook and video). St. Meinrad, IN: Abbey Press, 1996.

Tisdale, Leonora Tubs. *Preaching as Local Theology and Folk Art*. Minneapolis: Fortress Press, 1997.

Untener, Kenneth. *Preaching Better*. New York/Mahwah, NJ: Paulist Press, 1999.

USCCB. *New General Instruction on the Roman Missal*. Washington, DC: USCCB, 2003.

———. *Encuentro and Mission: A Renewed Pastoral Framework for Hispanic Ministry*. Bilingual Edition. Washington, DC: USCCB, 2002.

———. *Welcoming the Stranger Among Us: Unity in Diversity*. Washington, DC: USCCB, 2000.

———. *Strangers No Longer on the Journey of Hope*. Washington, DC: USCCB, 2003.

———. *Hispanic Ministry: Three Major Documents*. Washington, DC: USCCB, 1995.

———. "U.S. Bishops' Guidelines for Lay Preaching in Churches and Oratories." *Origins* 18, no. 25 (December 1, 1988): 402–4.

Wallace, James A., CSsR. *Preaching to the Hungers of the Heart: The Homily on the Feasts and Within the Rites*. Collegeville, MN: Liturgical Press, 2002.

————. "Guidelines for Preaching by the Laity: Another Step Backward?" *America* 161, no. 6 (September 9, 1989): 9–16.

————. *Imaginal Preaching: An Archetypal Perspective*. New York/Mahwah, NJ: Paulist Press, 1995.

Waznak, Robert P., SS. "Homily." In *The New Dictionary of Sacramental Worship*, ed. Peter E. Fink, SJ. Collegeville, MN: Liturgical Press, 1990, 552–58.

————. *Introduction to the Homily*. Collegeville, MN: Liturgical Press, 1998.

Willimon, William H., and Richard Lischer, eds. *Concise History of Preaching*. Louisville: Westminster John Knox Press, 1995.

Wilson, Lee, and Jason Moore. *Digital Story Tellers: The Art of Communicating the Gospel in Worship*. Nashville: Abingdon Press, 2002.

Wilson, Paul Scott. *The Practice of Preaching*, rev. ed. Nashville: Abingdon Press, 2007.

————. *The Four Pages of the Sermon*. Nashville: Abingdon Press, 1999.

————. *A Concise History of Preaching*. Nashville: Abingdon Press, 1992.

Wisdom, Andrew Carl, OP. *Preaching to a Multigenerational Assembly*. Collegeville, MN: Liturgical Press, 2004.

Zukowski, Angela Ann, and Pierre Babin, OMI. *The Gospel in Cyberspace: Nurturing Faith in the Internet Age*. Chicago: Loyola University Press, 2002.